PENGUIN BOOKS

THE DAO OF FLOW

Jin Young Lim is a PhD student at the Department of East Asian Languages and Cultural Studies at UC Santa Barbara. He was a Schwarzman Scholar class of '22 at Tsinghua University and Program Coordinator at the Berggruen Institute's China Center. Lim is the co-founder of Spawo Foundation, a non-profit dedicated to nurturing holistic education, sustainability, health and wellness, and culture in the Himalayas. He completed his undergraduate dual-degree from Waseda University and Peking University, majoring in liberal arts and international politics. He has led multiple mindfulness-based expeditions to the Himalayas and has been engaging in various contemplative practices throughout his life. During his free time, he moonlights as a writer, Taijiquan instructor, yoga teacher, Pu'er tea enthusiast, and content creator.

ADVANCE PRAISE FOR *THE DAO OF FLOW*

'Jin Young Lim in his monograph *The Dao of Flow* puts the flow of life itself with all of its vicissitudes at the center of the human experience. He illustrates with his own personal narrative—sometimes eventful, sometimes intellectual, sometimes anecdotal—how lives well-lived are a flow of video blogs that create their own storyline as they criss-cross and carry us from one intersection to the next. What Lim does in recounting his own adventures is to teach us how to inspire the everyday and transform what is most ordinary into the extraordinary. The life of Lim is surely what Francis Bacon meant when he declared that a person young in years can be old in hours if he has lost no time.'

—Roger T. Ames, philosopher and sinologist,
Humanities Chair Professor at Peking University

'Deep and flowing, this marvelous book brings the reader to peace and understanding by "bringing forth life", page after page. Part mémoire, part deep reflection, we discover the pathless path into our own lives as water finds its level, its depth, its way.'

—Roshi Joan Halifax, Abbot, Upaya Zen Center, author of
Standing at the Edge: Finding Freedom
Where Fear and Courage Meet

'A river of experiences—filled with love, peace, and open hearts. Water's journey, from icy peaks to the vast oceans, mirrors our humane path of nourishment, resilience, and compassion. This book reinforces the need to learn from nature and ancient wisdom.'

—Sonam Wangchuk, Inventor of Ice Stupa,
engineer, education reformist, and founder of
Himalayan Institute of Alternative Ladakh (HIAL)

'*The Dao of Flow* is a profound book. As a kindred spirit, I resonate with what Jin Young writes and find in the pages much to think about and learn. In his wide range of experiences, he discerns the wondrous manifestations of the Dao. That he should be able to do this as a young man is remarkable. But perhaps I reflect the prejudice of age. This is not only a book to be read, it is one to return to from time to time for insights and for enjoyment.'

—George Yeo, Former Minister for
Foreign Affairs, Singapore

'Through his own life story and those of his mentors, Jin Young weaves a lovely narrative of how one can live in the modern world in ways that flow naturally with wisdom and compassion.'

—Chade-Meng Tan, philanthropist,
Google's former 'Jolly Good Fellow',
and international bestselling author of
Search Inside Yourself and *Joy on Demand*

'Jin Young Lim does a wonderful job of introducing the fundamental principles of Taoism in an engaging and personal way. The lessons in this book can help you create more balance, harmony, and perspective in your personal life. And yet the applications of these lessons and insights can help you in your professional life as well. Future leaders, for example, can benefit from cultivating patience, compassion, humility, and adaptability—key qualities for effective communication and leadership. Jin Young Lim is a great storyteller and the teachings found in the *Tao Te Ching* are presented in this book in a refreshing and memorable way. I highly recommend this book for students and professionals alike.'

—Garr Reynolds, bestselling author on
the art of presentation, *Presentation Zen*

The Dao
of Flow

A journey
to discover the ancient
wisdom of water

Jin Young Lim

PENGUIN BOOKS

An imprint of Penguin Random House

PENGUIN BOOKS

Penguin Books is an imprint of the Penguin Random House group of
companies whose addresses can be found at
global.penguinrandomhouse.com

Published by Penguin Random House SEA Pte Ltd
40 Penjuru Lane, #03-12, Block 2
Singapore 609216

First published in Penguin Books by Penguin Random House SEA 2024

ISBN 9789815162271

Typeset in Garamond by MAP Systems, Bengaluru, India

www.penguin.sg

Dedicated to:

David Holley
Stanzin Gurmet
Kinuko Umoto
& to all precious life, pulsing with vitality

Contents

前言

Introduction

'The Dao has no fixed location;
It abides within an accomplished mind.
When the heart is still, and the *qi* regulated,
The Dao can thereby remain.
The Dao is not in the far distant,
It is what bears life to people.
Stray not from the Dao
And people shall attain harmony and wisdom.'

—*Guanzi* c. 350 BCE[1]

This book is a meditation on the Dao 道, or the 'Way', of Flow in my life. It is a partial memoir, a narrative of 'walking flowers'—people whom I adore and respect—and a treatise on Eastern philosophy. In writing this book, I have attempted to marry these three components by following a new paradigm that goes beyond the usual genre. I beg your forgiveness if you find it confusing when at times I oscillate back and forth between my own personal stories and those of others, interspersed with Daoist teachings,

---

[1] 「凡道無所, 善心安愛, 心靜氣理, 道乃可止。彼道不遠, 民得以產。彼道不離, 民因以知 (和)。」《管子・內業》. All translations in the main text are the author's own unless otherwise noted.

xi

quotes, or Zen riddles. It is intentional, and meant to better illuminate the shared principles behind various experiences and stories. For me, the Dao shouldn't be something up in the sky. It should be felt close to the bones and deep in one's heart. Perhaps the more we empty our mind, the more it becomes visible and applicable to our lives. As my teacher Roger Ames would say, it is '*shengsheng* 生生'—it brings forth life—it is a philosophy that is alive, dynamic, and regenerative.

The idea for this book came suddenly one morning after finishing my taijiquan (tai chi chuan) practice, which for now we can perhaps think of as a form of Chinese yoga. I quickly penned down some thoughts that expanded over time into more than a dozen modules. Over 2,500 years ago, Thales of Miletus, the ancient Greek mathematician-philosopher, came to the proposition that 'water' is the *archê*—the beginning, source, or principle—of all things. This belief, according to Aristotle, was acquired through his observation of the natural world, such as the moistness of seeds that give birth to living beings. Around the same era, in ancient China, one finds in the *Laozi*:[2]

> The supreme good is like regulating water (*shangshan zhishui* 上善治水)
> for water benefits myriad things,
> yet it is equanimous.[3]

The symbolic meaning of water as a nourishing essence or source of life seems to have cut across time, distance, and civilization to inspire developments in science and philosophy. My own intuitive

---

[2] The text *Laozi* is also famously known as *Tao Te Ching* (pinyin: *Daodejing*). Throughout this book, I try to adhere to Pinyin convention for transliterations from Chinese to English.

[3] 「上善治（似）水。水善利萬物而有靜（不爭），居眾之所惡，故幾於道矣。」《长沙马王堆帛书老子甲乙本合订校订本》This version of *Laozi* is from the Mawangdui text.

understanding of the Dao, derived from my taijiquan practice, has led me to propose three esoteric principles in life that relate to the quality of water. They are represented by three Chinese characters, each with its accompanying explication:

1. 松 (*song*): the state of embodying water
2. 流 (*liu*): the way of flowing water
3. 治 (*zhi*): the art of regulating water

I will explain more in the following chapters. But throughout this book, you will see these three principles recurring in various forms: in the mastery of various contemplative traditions—martial arts, yoga, meditation, tea, calligraphy, painting, and farming; in the transformation of one's body and mind; in the stories of historical figures and contemporary leaders who accomplished the seemingly impossible; in the way of life of indigenous communities; and in the heart and actions of individuals whose microcosmic Dao resonates with the grand scheme of macrocosmic Dao. When these principles are beautifully executed, the end result is unanimously 'harmonious' (*he* 和) and 'pleasurable' (*le* 樂)—a sense of agreement, long-lasting joy, and fulfilment.

In the first chapter of this book, these principles are traced back to Gun-Yu Mythology, an ancient Chinese folklore that juxtaposes the inefficacy of brute force against the path of skilful non-resistance—the Dao of Flow. According to a legend that has been passed down for millennia, Gun's method of building dikes and barricades failed in trying to solve the flood crisis along the Yellow River because he was trying hard to resist the force of water. In contrast to that, his son, Yu the Great, later succeeded in taming the flood because he embraced the force of water and aided rivers in flowing and expanding, thus nourishing Mother Earth and allowing the fruitful growth of crops and communities. The former reflects human ignorance, and an urge to exploit and control. The latter illuminates wisdom and humility—of respecting, emulating, and placing humanity within Nature rather than apart from it. Whether the legend is true or not, Yu the Great's methodology provides a powerful framework for embodying, flowing, and regulating 'water' that ultimately leads to the 'unification of heaven and humankind' (*tianren heyi* 天人合一).

This three-step framework is not so distanced from us. It can be found and applied in almost any situation. The 'water' serves as a metaphor for cultivated wisdom and compassion, as well as the antithesis of resistance or brute force. Upon mastery, the means and results are often felt and described as 'flow'. What was once difficult and challenging can now be achieved with ease and grace, like practising taijiquan. At this point, everything seems to happen on its own, like moving clouds and flowing water (*xingyun liushui* 行雲流水). Daoists call this state *wuwei* 無為 'non-action', 'non-exertion', or 'effortless action'. As noted in *Sunzi*:

> That the velocity of cascading water can send boulders bobbing about is due to its strategic advantage (*shi* 勢). That a bird of prey when it strikes can smash its victim to pieces is due to its timing.[4]

Thus, the crux of every situation is to figure out its unique *shi* 勢—the right skilful means, propensity, or strategic advantage—that will lead to an effortless flow. Even though an eagle may seem effortless in swooping down to grab its prey, its initial effort lies in taking flight and soaring through the sky to develop a bird's-eye view of its surroundings. In other words, *wuwei* is attained not through complete idleness but rather through a process of continuous inner cultivation, so that one can develop the wisdom and ability to steer and guide the path of development based

---

[4] 「激水之疾，至于漂石者，勢也。鷙鳥之擊，至于毀折者，節也。」
《勢篇・孫子兵法》Roger Ames' translation.

on the appropriate *shi* (*yinshi lidao* 因勢利導). When people are able to embody the Dao, they tend to see all things as equal and may have enhanced ability to respond spontaneously and harmoniously to whatever situation may arise. Like water, they are flexible in their approach in handling each unique circumstance without resistance.

Some may mistake this harmony or non-resistance for passivity. But *wuwei* is no more passive than a river. Indeed, the wisdom of water has made its way into martial arts (Bruce Lee famously urged his students to be 'shapeless, formless, like water') precisely because the concepts of flow, harmony, and non-resistance become powerful forces for action when wielded by a wise and practised master. I hope readers of this book will learn valuable lessons from the relationship between the non-resistant *wuwei* and the strategic *shi* and find new ways in our world to apply this wisdom for positive action.

The more I meditate on early Daoist philosophy and continue on my personal contemplative training, the more I come to perceive the Dao of Flow in the lives of several of my role models. These individuals were able to rise above their 'ego-self' and pierce into the nature of a problem to come up with a harmonious big-picture solution. They were in the truest sense 'Daoist alchemists'.

I recall my first visit to Japan as a volunteer, where I met Koyu Abe, a Japanese Zen priest who spent more than a decade trying to decontaminate Fukushima's radiation after the 2011 tsunami and nuclear meltdown. This encounter, which I named as the *Kizuna* 絆 experience—a kanji character representing human bond or interconnectedness—led me to studying abroad in Japan and China, and to start a non-profit in Ladakh, India. In these places, I had the good fortune to learn from countless individuals and mentors. David Holley, a retired *Los Angeles Times* foreign correspondent-turned-professor who has now retreated to the countryside of Japan as a hobby farmer, skilfully flowed the spirit of curiosity and non-attachment, integrity, and compassion in both his journalistic writing and teaching career. Venerable Sanghasena showed me the vastness of human potential, the magic of transforming a 250-acre desert land on top of the Himalayas into a holistic educational hub surrounded by an oasis of vibrant community. And Scott Rozelle, a Stanford experimental economist in China demonstrated how a deep understanding of local history, geography, and customs informed his approach to design-based research and intervention to improve China's rural education. While these are just to name a few, there were many more who—through their own actions—inspired me to contemplate, discern, and hopefully, manifest Daoist wisdom in my own life.

Through a cup of tea, I discovered the Dao of Flow thriving in the lives of indigenous tribes living in the protected Yunnan tea mountains, which made me question the notion of modern development and challenge the unsustainable model of global capitalism. A visit to an organic farming village in Japan invited me to further explore the incredible work of Fukuoka Masanobu, a Japanese farmer who famously 'farmed without farming,' doing 'nothing' and yet, in what at first seems like unfathomable success, produced an abundance of yield through the power of Nature. How is that possible? And what is the secret behind Masanobu's approach? I hope the Dao of Flow can better inform our understanding of agriculture and a more sustainable society in addition to many other things.

Back in Beijing, I delved into the life story of Professor Lü Zhi, a panda-researcher and wildlife biologist who spent decades shadowing giant pandas, snow leopards, and other endangered animals in the wild. Having witnessed China's economic reforms and its impact on the natural environment, she examined and utilized various economic and cultural incentives to help inspire local villagers to participate in biodiversity conservation. Today, her foundation Shan Shui continues to work with universities, indigenous groups, businesses, and the Chinese government to develop science-based conservation and ecological practices in both rural and urban settings.

While studying as a Schwarzman Scholar at Tsinghua University, I also discovered Zhuangzi's playful wandering spirit embodied in the famed Chinese artist Han Meilin, known for designing the famous Fuwa Dolls for the 2008 Beijing Olympics. Less known to the world, Han was tortured and persecuted during the Cultural Revolution. Yet, his love for animals and the local peasants not only sustained his life, but invigorated his designs and drawings. Even after his mid-80s, Han Meilin's lifelong collection and research of undeciphered ancient Chinese characters continued to inspire his creation of *Tianshu*, the 'Heavenly Script', which he applied to his painting, calligraphy, ceramics, wood carving, and other art work.

Finally, the Dao of Flow comes full circle with the story of Nakamura Tetsu, a Japanese physician-turned-hydrologist who spent his life trying to shine light on a corner of the world by saving lives in war-torn Afghanistan. Nakamura's Dao of building canals in the Kunar region—of embodying, flowing, and regulating water—resembles that of Yu the Great. It also stands in juxtaposition to the United States' foreign policy of periodically trying to implement democracy by military brute force. Much like Gun's approach of building barricades and resistances, the United States' foreign policy in the Middle East backfired miserably. Hundreds of thousands of civilians and soldiers died from the War on Terror, and US veterans who returned from Afghanistan are still suffering from trauma. In contrast, even after Nakamura's passing, his waterway projects continue to bring light and peace to the local region, benefitting more than a million people. His spirit is still alive, flowing and enriching the lives of many volunteers who worked under him. Among Nakamura's many protégés, I managed to have a lovely conversation with Hasuoka Osamu, a social educator who worked to propagate peace in Japan through picture-book storytelling after returning from Afghanistan.

The effect of a well-regulated flow is *yun* 韻, a 'harmonizing after-effect'—a concept to describe a spiritual, strong, ever-lasting imprint in one's consciousness after experiencing something powerful yet uniquely harmonious. As I try to demonstrate in this book, *yun* is found in a cup of delicate Pu'er tea, in a magnificent calligraphy artwork, in a well-trained martial artist, and in the lives of countless individuals who embodied, flowed, and regulated their lives like water.

This book is an invitation to be a 'walking flower', to walk the Dao of Flow in your own life and to embody the wisdom of water.

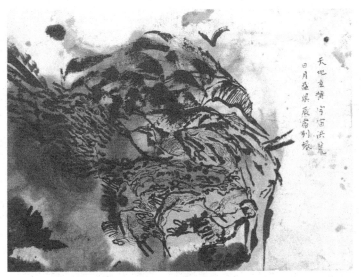

Author's collaborative artwork with Azul Pereda

Heaven was dark-cyan, Earth grey-yellow,
time and space vast and boundless.
The sun rises and falls, the moon wanes and waxes,
infinite stars orderly filled the open sky.
—*The Thousand Character Classic*

Prologue

不求甚解

Catch any Useful Message, and Forget the Stories

'Dear friends, I would like to share a story with you. Some of you might have heard it before. It is quite a modern one, and I'm worried that you clever people might think too much about it. Don't overthink as such, "oh, how can this story be true? This monk must be fooling us with some cock-and-bull story." Yes, the story may not be true. But true or not, every story has a message. Someone is trying to show you a beautiful moon in the sky by pointing their finger at it. If you keep fixating your gaze on their finger, you will never catch even the tiniest glimpse of the moon. And if you see the moon, there is no need to hold on to the finger forever. Let go of it, and enjoy the moon. In the same way, catch my message, and forget the story.'

Surreal as it may seem, we are sitting on the peak of a mountain in the Himalayas with one of the wisest and most compassionate teachers in my life. Overlooking the mountain range, Venerable Sanghasena, a social-reformer and Buddhist monk, is imparting words of wisdom before giving us a short guided meditation. He pauses for a moment and continues with his story.

'A long, long time ago, back in the old days, when human beings were yet to be born on Earth, this planet was so beautiful, so pure, and clean. We can imagine there was no air pollution, water pollution, or plastics. No Coca Cola and Pepsi Cola. No diabetes. It was full of pretty flowers, tall trees, and green mountains. So beautiful, that God thought: "Oh my, this Mother Earth is so beautiful, something is missing. Why shouldn't I create a few human beings who can live on this planet and enjoy this beautiful nature, the flowers, this sunshine, the moonlight, and rivers?"

'With this intention in mind, God created a few human beings, and he said to them: "My dear human beings, this world is so beautiful. Look around you, there used to be no one to enjoy them. But now I've created you to live in peace, love, and goodwill with one another. Go, my friend. Go and enjoy the beauty of sunrise and sunset. Smell the roses, climb some trees, and explore the mountains. Go, sing, dance, and play with the wonders of life."

'"Thanks, Lord", they bowed and scattered off.

'The next day, in the morning, somebody came knocking at His door. Yawning and waking up from bed, God was puzzled. "Hmmm, this is early, who could it be?" This had never happened before, and as he opened the door, a few human beings, whom he had just created yesterday, stood in front of him and started complaining about each other: "God, he is such a jerk . . . she insulted me this way . . ." and so on so forth.

'God said, "What?! What am I hearing now? Not even a day has passed and how dare you complain about one another. Have I not told you to live in peace, love, and goodwill? Never complain or fight with each other. Go and enjoy this beautiful nature. Go, my friend. Go, sing, dance, and celebrate the gift of nature."

'"Okay, Lord," they said, and off they went.

'The following morning, a little earlier than yesterday, the human beings returned and knocked at God's door, a little louder this time. God wondered, *Wow, who else could it be today?* To his surprise, he saw the same few fellows he had created two days ago, this time, complaining about one another with even greater intensity. "Not only did she say this to me, but she also did this to me . . . Not only did he insult me, but he also attacked me . . ." the humans cried and argued.

"'Oh my God! What is this?" God exclaimed.

"'This is only the second day. And how dare you still complain and fight with each other. Have I not told you that I've created you to live in peace, love, and goodwill? Go sing, dance, and enjoy the wonders of nature. Never quarrel, never fight, never complain. Never come to me again. I am telling you."

"'Okay, Lord," and off the humans went.

'Well, you guessed it right. The same thing happened again and again for the next couple of days, and God's quaint-looking door was on the verge of breaking. Even before he opened the door, God knew who was behind it. He fully realized that nobody else could be paying him a kind visit, none other than the few annoying human beings whom he'd created a few days ago.

"'Neither are these human beings going to live in peace nor are they going to allow me to live in peace. What a big mistake I've made. Being a creator, I cannot kill them. But I'm sure now that they are going to continue complaining, quarrelling, and fighting against each other. What should I do?" In that moment, God called an emergency meeting of his ministers.

"'My dear ministers, I'm in serious trouble. I need your help."

"'Oh God, please do not joke. It doesn't sound funny."

"'No, no joke. I'm serious. I mean it."

"'How? You're God! If you're in deep water, what about us? How can *you* be in trouble? We don't understand. Please explain."

'God explained the whole story to his ministers. How he saw the beauty of this world, what he thought, and how he created a few human beings who ended up being a nuisance as they knew nothing but to complain and fight.

"'Now these humans are not playing guitars and flutes, but are making guns and throwing bombs at each other! They are not dancing and singing, but are fighting and killing one another. Oh my, I've made a terrible mistake. And I've failed to convince them to live in peace, love, and goodwill; in fact, the more I try to convince them, the more atrocities they commit under my name! So now I need your help . . . to find a place where I can hide from these human beings!"

'The ministers whispered among themselves. And one by one, a few stood up to give their opinions.

"'Lord, very easy."

"'What? What is it?"

"'Why don't you move to the top of Mt. Everest? It is so cold there, and there is no oxygen. No one can go up there."

'God thought for a while and said: "No, no, it is not a safe place. Tenzin Norgay and Edmund Hillary will eventually reach the top of Everest, I foresee."

"'Well, very easy, sir."

"'What?"

"'Why don't you hide in the depths of the ocean? There is no way human beings can survive there."

"'No, no, it is not safe either. These human beings will soon carry something on their back (an oxygen tank), connect something to their mouth, and find a way to reach the bottom of the sea."

"'What about the moon, sir? It must be the safest place! Away from Earth!"

'Again, God thought for a while, and said, "Oh no no, this is not a safe place. This American guy Neil Armstrong will soon find a way to reach the moon and find me!"

'After a brief hush, one very old minister with a long beard stood up and whispered into the ear of God.

"'God, why don't you hide in the hearts of human beings themselves. They will be searching for you everywhere. They will be searching for you in space, in the ocean, on the moon, and up in the Himalayas. They will be searching for you in holy places like Jerusalem, mosques, temples, and churches.

They will be searching for you in the holy books and saints, they will even fight against one another thinking they will find you after death. They will be searching far and wide, but they will never think of looking within themselves to find you. And even if they do find you in their heart, assuming there would be a few smart humans indeed, they must have been the ones who have lived in peace, love, harmony, and goodwill. And they shall not bother you."

'God was silent for a while and then he whispered back, "Shhh, please keep it confidential, don't tell it to anyone! Thank you, my wise friend, and, bye bye!"

'The story has it that since then, God has been hiding in the hearts of mankind. So, dear friends, whatever you're looking for, heaven, hell, God or ghost, Buddha or Mara, here (Sanghasena pointing to his heart), right here is where you should be looking. The way to look for it, in yogic terminology, is through "meditation". Meditation is the way to turn our outward-seeking attention inward. This is not easy, for we have been trained since childhood to look further and further away, run faster, think deeper, work harder, and possess more things even if we don't need them. This is how we've been conditioned and educated. And now, meditation is the reverse of this. It is the deconditioning of your habits. Stop thinking, stop running, and stop searching. Just arrive here, and be quiet, be still with your heart. And who knows, you might find God within. For me, God is not a figure sitting on the golden throne up in heaven looking at us. God is universal love, pure compassion, and wisdom. It is a state to be experienced in your heart. So let us now attempt to move one step closer to the core of our being. With this, I invite you to soften your gaze and sit comfortably and peacefully as we begin our meditation.'

This book is a meditation on the Dao of Flow.

Catch any useful messages, and forget the stories if they are not helpful.

Ven. Sanghasena sharing stories of wisdom and compassion
on the top of Mahabodhi's Heavenly Hill in Ladakh

This book is divided into four parts, each represented by a character from the four-character idiomatic expression *xingyun liushui* 行雲流水 (Moving Clouds, Flowing Water)

Part I

Xing 行

Way-Making

行 雲 流 水

Chapter One

大禹

Yu the Great

'To be bestowed by *Tian* (Heaven or Nature) with great responsibility,

one must toughen the mind and determination,

workout the sinews and bones,

fast the body and flesh,

empty one's self,

and be ready to face unexpected outcomes.

Those whose heart is vitalized and who can endure with grit,

shall grow beyond their limits.'

—Mencius[1]

About 2,000 years before the common era, a boy by the name of Wenming was born in modern-day Sichuan into an era of great suffering. This was a period of time known as the Great Flood when China was plagued by torrential rains, storms, and prolonged famine. Exodus was a common thing as people had to

---

[1] 「故天將降大任於是人也，必先苦其心志，勞其筋骨，餓其體膚，空乏其身，行拂亂其所為，所以動心忍性，曾益其所不能。」《孟子·告子下》

constantly move their homes around, juggling between the safety of living on higher grounds and the benefits of living near the river valley basin, which was more conducive for agriculture yet exposed to the danger of flood.

Wenming's father, Gun, was an engineer of his time appointed by Emperor Yao to seek a solution that would solve the outburst of floods along the Yellow River that originates in the eastern plateau of Tibet in the Bayan Har mountains, runs through the central heartland, and exits into the Bohai Sea. Wenming grew up witnessing the efforts of his father experimenting with different methods to mitigate the flood crisis around China's greatest rivers. His father had devised a system of containment by building dikes and dams along the rivers to hold the water using *xirang*—a self-renewing soil with the special ability to stretch and expand on its own to counter the rising water level. According to legend, Gun either found or created this magical substance, or stole it from heaven.[2] After nine years of expansive hard work, Gun thought he was making significant progress but a major flood came toppling all the tall barricades he built, which upon collapsing poured forth massive destruction, killing thousands of people.

Failing in his mission, Gun was banished by the newly crowned Emperor Shun to the outskirts of Feather Mountain, where he eventually died. By this time, Wenming, already a fine young man, was spared and given a chance to revise his father's methodology—to right what went wrong. On the fourth day of his marriage, he received an order from Emperor Shun to take over his father's role as the new hydrologist and immediately set off to work. After bidding farewell to his beloved wife, Wenming departed on a long journey throughout the country.

---

[2] Lihui Yang, Deming An, and Jessica Anderson Turner, *Handbook of Chinese Mythology* (New York: Oxford University Press, 2008), p. 218.

His first instinct was to try and find out the root problem of the crisis by studying the geography and socio-demographics of the region.

Growing up on the slopes of Mount Song, just south of the Yellow River, Wenming had spent most of the formative period of his life listening to his father's stories and observing the river flow from above. He had seen how, depending on the seasons and weather, a river can erratically change from what seemed like the joyful skipping of a quiet gentle lady to the wrathful uproar of a hungry demon ready to devour its prey. When the current is tame, a river is kind and soft, providing nature's gift to mankind— sufficient water to nourish the earth and trees, and at the same time allowing all kinds of human activities to be carried out in its soft embrace. When the current is too strong, everything is swept away and nothing seems capable of obstructing its way. Regardless, a river only flows downhill, never uphill. That is the river's nature. One thing that Wenming realized from his father's mistakes was that the more you try to resist or block the flow of water, whether through the use of dikes or dams, the more the volume of liquid and energy you trap in a reservoir of water, which, upon reaching a tipping point, might unleash an even greater force that is indomitable.

Could the solution perhaps lie in finding a way to divert the flow of a river's current? What if people could find a way to maintain the volume and speed of the water at a rate that is manageable and comfortable for people? These were some of the questions he had in mind.

As he travelled from place to place, Wenming continued to observe Mother Nature. He drew charts of creeks, and maps of forests, valleys, and mountains. He noted every curve, winding, and meander that was formed along a river and observed where flooding was frequent. Everywhere he went, he shared his aspiration with people from different tribes and united them as one. His benign presence and humility touched the hearts of many. With the help of the wise Emperor Shun, they divided the land into nine provinces and coordinated people towards creating a new holistic system of crisis control derived from his observation of the downward-flowing nature of rivers. This included a nationwide effort digging out irrigation canals to channel water from the upper and middle course rivers into fields and plains; connecting watercourses from the nine great rivers into the sea; and dredging riverbeds to remove excess sediment to ensure a smoother flow of water. There were times when he integrated some of his father's methods in building dikes and levees when deemed necessary. The general principle was to keep water moving at a pace in harmony with heaven and earth. When there was a noticeable rise in river water, canals were opened up, and like shepherds tending to their sheep, farmers carefully directed the flow of water into empty spaces. This was a rare moment in history when different tribesmen were unified, working collectively towards a shared common goal.

Wenming vowed to not return home until he succeeded in taming the flood. His massive hydraulic work ended up consuming the prime of his youth, during which he spent most of his time eating, sleeping, and working with the common workers. Some said that he happened to pass by his house's doorstep three times, but chose not to enter despite hearing the wailing of his newborn son. His hands and feet were thickly callused, his skin tanned and burned, yet his spirit never once wavered under the scorching sun.

> With ragged clothes and poor diet, he paid his devotions to the spirits until his wretched hovel fell in the ditch . . . on the one hand, he used the marking-line, and on the other the compass and square . . . He made the roads communicable, banked up the marshes, surveyed the hills, [and taught the

common people] that paddies should be planted in low damp places.[3]

After thirteen years of zealous hardship, the rivers were finally tamed, and the Great Flood came to an end. Emperor Shun was so impressed with Wenming's calibre and integrity, that he appointed him as the prime minister and later abdicated his throne in favour of Wenming as the next successor to rule the country. Wenming was given the name Emperor Yu, more commonly known as *Da Yu* 大禹, meaning 'Yu The Great', and would go on to live until the age of 108—establishing the Xia Dynasty—the first dynasty in China's history.

This folktale, known as the 'Gun-Yu Mythology' or 'Great Yu Tames the Flood' (*dayu zhishui* 大禹治水), has been passed down in East Asia for millennia. In China, it has been taught in elementary school textbooks as a lesson on ethics and morality, encouraging students to persevere in the face of obstacles by showing them how their ancient ancestors had endured and prevailed in the face of unprecedented calamities. Motifs, historical sites, and cultural worship of Yu the Great can be found across China, Japan, and Korea.

Wang Min, a professor at Hosei University has researched and written extensively on the influence of Emperor Yu in Japan in her book *Yu the Great and the Japanese: East Asia Linked by the Sage-King Who Controlled the Flood Waters*. She tracked down shrines in

---

[3] Herbert J. Allen, 'Ssŭma Ch'ien's Historical Records. Chapter II', *Journal of the Royal Asiatic Society of Great Britain and Ireland*, (1895), pp. 93–110, http://www.jstor.org/stable/25197242. Original line: 「禹乃遂与益、后稷奉帝命, 命诸侯百姓兴人徒以傅土, 行山表木, 定高山大川。禹伤先人父鲧功之不成受诛, 乃劳身焦思, 居外十三年, 过家门不敢入。薄衣食, 致孝于鬼神。卑宫室, 致费于沟淢。陆行乘车, 水行乘船, 泥行乘橇, 山行乘檋。左准绳, 右规矩, 载四时, 以开九州, 通九道, 陂九泽, 度九山。令益予众庶稻, 可种卑湿。命后稷予众庶难得之食。食少, 调有馀相给, 以均诸侯。禹乃行相地宜所有以贡, 及山川之便利。」

Japan that were dedicated to Yu the Great, and the role of an
Emaki painting, found on the sliding doors of Kyoto's imperial
palace, depicting Emperor Yu swearing off alcohol, serving as a
reminder for Japanese emperors to avoid excessive indulgence and
to strive for the benefits of their people. Alongside the legendary
Five Emperors, Yu the Great was regarded as a sage-king, a
paragon of leadership for many East Asian rulers. What he set was
an ideal example of a wise and virtuous ruler who rose beyond
one's personal interest in favour of the nation. He was respected
for ending chaos, restoring peace, and bringing prosperity to his
people. The multifaceted flood control system that Yu devised not
only helped reduce the suffering of people by taming the vicious
floods that had inundated ancient China for many generations
but also improved transportation, infrastructure, agriculture, and
relations between people. As more and more people settled down
in permanent villages along the Yellow River, Chinese civilization
began to grow and flourish.

Of course, Yu the Great was not a man without flaws.
He was, after all, like us, a human being. One could argue
that he was probably not a good husband or father due to his
prolonged absence; or that he was violent for allegedly executing
a chieftain for being late to an important meeting. Some people
even thought him questionable for passing on the throne to his
own son after his death, which led to the discontinuation of the
noble *shanrang* 禪讓 system—a tradition of former sage-kings
passing on their throne to whom they regard as most deserving,
not due to bloodline but because of high moral conduct and
competence. That being said, it is quite remarkable that Yu
the Great was equally acknowledged by the early philosophers
and thinkers from ancient China, be it Confucianism, Mohism,
Legalism, or Daoism.

He was lauded by Confucius for having lived minimally and
for setting up an efficient bureaucracy based on 'proper order'
(*li* 理). Yu the Great was mentioned as many as fifty-six times

in the book *Mozi* 墨子 for applying scientific rationality and technology, practising austerity, and embodying 'universal love'—three of the main values promulgated by the Mohists. Legalists would commend his strict enforcement of the law, as shown in his consolidation of state power, the establishment of the Xia dynasty government, and the division of China into nine administrative regions. And finally, Daoists would point to Yu's approach of taming the flood—by channelling river waters into fields and oceans—as the epitome of emulating the *Dao*, the Way of Heaven, Earth, and Humanity (*tian di ren* 天地人) because his actions were derived from the careful observation and understanding of nature. The *Daodejing* espouses that:

> Humanity emulates Earth,
> Earth emulates Heaven,
> Heaven emulates the Dao,
> and the Dao emulates what is natural.[4]

Above all, the Gun-Yu mythology reveals an alternative way of being, a methodology that is based on 'adaptability and unobstructed-ness' (*biantong* 變通). The *Yijing* (Book of Changes) says:

> When exhausted, adapt to change (*bian* 變);
> change in order to remain unobstructed (*tong* 通);
> and by remaining unobstructed, one endures.[5]

I call this wisdom the Dao of Flow. When faced with struggles, our instinctive ego reaction is to fight or flight—to want and control, exploit, and force our will on others. This habitual pattern is often ineffective. But according to the ancient sages, it is transcendable

---

[4] 「人法地，地法天，天法道，道法自然。」《老子》
[5] 「易窮則變，變則通，通則久。」《周易・繫辭下》

through self-cultivation. As I will try to demonstrate in later chapters, one can try to emulate the natural laws of nature much like Yu did, by learning to 'embody, flow, and regulate water' in various situations and circumstances in order to achieve a harmonious end goal—regardless of whether one is a student, an entrepreneur, a teacher, an activist, or the leader of a country.

Has one lived a good life? It is hard to say, for it can only be revealed at our deathbed whether it was good, bad, happy, sad, or most likely a mixture of all. The famous Athenian statesman Solon once told King Croesus to 'count no man happy until the end is known'. Despite things going swimmingly today, nobody knows for sure what the gods may bring tomorrow. Suppose that Yu the Great succeeded in taming the Great Flood during his lifetime, which was a tremendous success in history, however, he did not and could not eliminate the possibility of floods happening in the future. Rivers do not stop running, and sediments continue to build up in the riverbed on a daily basis. This is the law of impermanence, and that is why we need to continuously adapt and flow—*biantong*.

Manmade canals accumulate silt over time and are rendered useless if they are not well-maintained. As ephemeral as anything else in this world, nature will continue to shift and transform every single day. The Yellow River, for instance, has changed its course across the plains several times, each time bringing deadly floods and famines that killed millions. This phenomenon was seen and recorded during the Yuan and Qing dynasty and again in the twentieth century, with the most recent destructive flood happening in 1931, inundating 34,000 square miles of land and displacing eighty million people, leaving close to four million dead in China.

Ongoing efforts and change are required not just to create peace and prosperity, but also to maintain it. Nature, God, the universe, karma, whatever one calls it, seems to be constantly testing our individual grit as well as our collective strength in the face of new adversities. Thus, the merits of an organization, a dynasty, a nation, or a civilization should be measured from its inception till its very end; and the quality of an individual's life should be measured over the course of their entire life. Perhaps Yu the Great has led a 'good life' so much so that his name and deeds continue to live on in the celebrated memories of people long after his passing. This wisdom, the Dao of Flow, in which he was able to tap into thousands of years ago is still very much alive today, and it awaits our discovery.

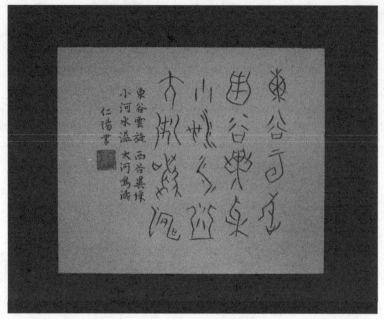

Author's oracle bone script calligraphy artwork

In the eastern vale, clouds swirl and dance
The western valley reveals a medley of colours
Little streams brim with water
Great rivers splash and roar

Chapter Two

格物

Observing the Pattern

'Since ancient times
Those who want to illuminate virtue all under heaven
first keep their state in peace.
Wanting to regulate the state well,
they first harmonize their family.
Wanting to harmonize their family,
they first cultivate themselves.
Wanting to cultivate the self, they first align their heart.
Wanting to align their heart, they first purify thoughts.
Wanting to purify thoughts,
they first acquire deep understanding or awareness.
Wanting to acquire deep understanding or awareness,
They must first and foremost observe and inspect [the patterns
of] myriad things.'

—*The Great Learning* by Confucius[1]

---

[1] 「古之欲明明德於天下者，先治其國。欲治其國者，先齊其家，欲齊其家者，先修其身。欲修其身者，先正其心。欲正其心者，先誠其意。欲誠其意者，先致其知。致知在格物。」《禮記・大學》

13

Throughout history, humans have been trying to make sense of our existence in this world. Without a single hint, warning, or any explanations we were brought into this world—into a country, a culture, and a family that was not the by-product of our free will. Why are we here? What is the meaning of our life? And where are we heading to? These are some of the existential questions that have plagued humanity since the dawn of time.

Five thousand years have passed since Yu's taming of the flood in China. Things have changed drastically on many fronts. Nation-states, global conglomerates, and international organizations have emerged. As I'm writing, new technologies are being invented each day and we're going through a new digital revolution, perhaps an Artificial Intelligence (AI) revolution. Life has indeed improved for most of humanity, as Steven Pinker made the case in his book *The Better Angels of Our Nature*, violence and extreme poverty have declined over the past century, 'honestly, this is the safest time to be alive!' However, the nature of reality remains the same. So is human nature. We still live in a capricious world full of colours and chaos, love and cruelty, joy and suffering, yin and yang, and still a world based on our individual perception and subjective experience. No matter how much things have changed externally, our personal world still revolves around our consciousness, and the planets still revolve around the sun. Modern science can help alleviate pain, but it doesn't eliminate suffering. Pleasure can be fed, but happiness can only to be found within. Our new economy may offer various job opportunities to make ends meet, but it doesn't ensure fulfilment nor does it quench our thirst to discover the true purpose of our life.

The core philosophy of this book is built on several premises. One, as we've mentioned, is that Yu the Great has led a 'good life' worthy of examination and emulation. His approach is a close approximation of the Dao of Flow, just as how Taijiquan practitioners repeat their forms every single day to perfect their movements by copying those of their teacher. Even the teacher, a highly accomplished master, is still striving to approximate 'the perfect form of Taiji', which is akin to the movement of flowing water. A perfect form or a perfect way is theoretically unattainable, yet we do have a close-to-perfection model as a reference guide that can be passed down from one generation to the next. And maybe such imperfection is perfect! The *Daodejing* (aka *Tao Te Ching*) is one shining example, which in its opening lines states that—'The Dao that can be told is not the eternal Dao', yet it doesn't deter Laozi[2] from trying to explain the Dao, and the *Daodejing* still ends up becoming one of the most influential Classic texts on Chinese spirituality. Keeping that in mind, if we examine the meaning and purpose of human existence from Yu's mythology, we can draw several inferences. The first one, I suggest, is:

> The core purpose of our life is to maintain inner and outer harmony while striving to actualize our potential as human beings. It is when our body, mind, and heart are aligned with a higher cause—a personal cause that is unique yet, when brought to its final completion, fits harmoniously into a bigger picture to fill up a missing puzzle.

The word *harmony* is key here. It is the central tenet of this path as well as the fruition. One's body, mind, and heart must be in harmony with the initial intentions, the overall actions, and ideally the final results of what they are pursuing. But how do we define harmony? Let's take a brief look at the etymology of 'harmony' as well as its equivalent meaning in *kanji*—the character 和— pronounced as *he* in Chinese and *wa* in Japanese.

---

[2] The *Daodejing* is traditionally attributed to Laozi, a semi-legendary ancient Chinese philosopher, but the authorship of this text has been debated. Here you may think of it as the author(s) of this text.

In English, the word harmony was derived from Greek *harmonia*, meaning 'agreement, concord of sounds'.[3] *Harmonia* is achieved when different tones and musical instruments are combined and played simultaneously to produce chords that are pleasing to the ears. In a symphony orchestra, each musician of the concert band is responsible for playing their part of a notated musical score with an instrument that is uniquely theirs (a personal cause), one which they are inclined towards, with skill that they have practised and honed for perhaps tens of thousands of hours, before finally performing in front of an audience. Yet, when played simultaneously, the music that each individual produces overlaps with one another in an appealing and comfortable manner, fitting miraculously into this 'bigger picture' that we call a symphony (the higher cause). The musical moment created by an orchestra with a large ensemble composed of wind, string, brass, and percussion instruments played by a hundred musicians can be captivating, uplifting, and awe-inspiring. Despite the number of people and the diversity of instruments, there is no conflict or chaos. Just a sense of peace, order, and congruence. *Harmony* in its perfect sense brings joy and pleasure.

In the Chinese dictionary, we can find two common variant characters of *he* (和 ‧ 龢) for the word *harmony* that have the same meaning and are pronounced the same way but written differently.[4] Even though 和 is the dominant character used today in modern Mandarin due to its simplicity, both characters were used interchangeably in the past, and are still used in calligraphy.

龢 *he* = 龠 + 禾
和 *he* = 禾 + 口

---

[3] 'Harmony', Online Etymology Dictionary, https://www.etymonline.com/search?q=harmony.

[4] For more information, refer to 《康熙字典》 or 《說文解字》

With these two etymologies, we can further deduce that the origin of 和 · 龢 is connected to three elementary characters, which are explained below.

龠 *yue*
禾 *he*
口 *kou*

龠 (*yue*) is a kind of primitive flute-like woodwind instrument that originated during the Xia Dynasty and was incorporated into the ritual and music culture of ancient China. Archaeologists have unearthed some of the world's oldest playable flutes—the *Jiahu* bone flutes—in China dating back to about 9,000 years old.[5] In China, music is known to enrich one's spirit and help promote tolerance between different hierarchies or social groups, such as the relationships between governments and people, monarchs and officials, elders and youths, and also between clans or tribes. Music is a universal language of its own, one that transcends boundaries and verbal languages. Thus it seems like the earliest indication of 和 · 龢, much like its western cousin *harmonia* is related to the properties of music.

禾 (*he*) provides a fresh perspective of understanding 和 · 龢, which is found in both characters. Stand alone, it can represent 'foxtail millet', the first crop that was predominantly cultivated in China, or 'the five grains'—a grouping of five farmed crops that were considered important in ancient China: soybeans, wheat, broomcorn or barley, millet, and rice or hemp. As written earlier, the harnessing of water by Yu the Great brought about the large-scale domestication of crops that helped feed millions of people, allowing the population to grow. Note that these staple foods

---

[5] Juzhong Zhang et al., 'Oldest Playable Musical Instruments Found at Jiahu Early Neolithic Site in China', *Nature* 401, no. 6751 (September 1999): 366-68, doi:10.1038/43865.

are all vegetarian—their means of production require no animal slaughter. Thus, harmony, too, can be understood as the antithesis of violence and cruelty.

Besides that, the oracle bone script of 禾 resembles that of a ripe millet that was planted in spring and harvested in the eighth month of the lunar calendar, in autumn, at a time when it was 'just right' for reaping. In a way similar to Yu's taming of rivers, farmers must first understand the nature of crops in order to determine the perfect season for sowing the seeds and for collecting their harvest. This requires careful observation and experimentation to find out the right answers and the practice of moderation in abiding by nature's principles.

Last but not least, 口 (*kou*) is a pictogram of the human mouth, the organ that we use for eating and speaking. Do notice that 口 is also found within the character of 龠, which seems like a no-brainer since flutists have to use their mouth to blow streams of air into the mouth-hole of a flute to produce sounds. There's a common saying in China that an emperor should uphold his people as *tian*, heaven or utmost importance, and the common people regard food as their *tian*.[6]

Perhaps we can now conclude that the harmony of a society is built upon the stability and sufficiency of staple food to feed its people; it is an antithesis to violence, brutality, and conflicts, and requires the maintenance of peace through the practice of skilful communication and moderation. When in harmony, the state is akin to that of musical *harmonia* or *symphonia*.

I'm always amazed when it comes to the discovery of new word etymology, for it can reveal so much information about how our predecessors thought in the past, back in a time when words were still limited and when meanings were very much derived from our direct perception of reality. Time and again, these intuitive perceptions, told via the origin of a word, point us towards some form of pattern that is found in nature. By understanding

---

[6] 「王者以民為天，而民以食為天。」《新序・善謀下》

one pattern, for example, the definition of harmony in musical composition, we're provided with insights into other patterns of harmony in our lives because there seems to be an underlying Pattern—with a capital P—an organizing principle that connects everything in this world.

Plato calls it the Forms. Pythagoreans call it *Kosmos*—a universal world order they discovered through numbers, proportions, mathematics, geometry, and astronomy. The Daoists named it *Dao* 道. In Buddhism, it's *Dhamma* or Truth. Neo-confucianists call it *li* 理, oftentimes translated as coherence, or patterning.

In *Tao: The Watercourse Way*, Alan Watts described *li* as

> the asymmetrical, nonrepetitive, and unregimented order which we find in the patterns of moving water, the forms of trees and clouds, of frost crystals on the window, or the scattering of pebbles on beach sand.[7]

These patterns may seem random and diverse at first, however, they are manifested from some sort of shared organizing principle, a 'Metapattern' perhaps, as defined by anthropologist Gregory Bateson.

I once saw a satirical cartoon depicting a scientist using a microscope to examine the skin of an organism. By tweaking his device to magnify the image, he first saw the shapes of tissues, followed by cells, organelles, molecules, and all the way to the smallest particle we now know as an atom. And while he was busy examining the different levels of organization within this organism, he was completely oblivious that behind him, a larger eye was watching him from outside the window. And an even larger eye was watching from outside the universe. My initial reaction was sort of a mixture of intrigue and disturbance. I turned and looked out of my room's window, wondering if I, too, was being

---

[7] Alan Watts and Al Chung-liang Huang, *Tao: The Watercourse Way* (New York: Pantheon Books, 1975), p. 46.

watched. I guess there are many ways in which we could interpret this 'eye' behind us. Is it God? 'Big Brother'? or Mother Earth?

My own preferred way of interpretation—one that is less disturbing—is that this larger eye represents our family. Just as cells come together to form tissues and organs, individuals group as families, which further develop into societies, nations, civilizations, and collective humanity. This bigger eye that is watching us need not be strange, aggressive, or bizarre. It does not need to be aliens spying on us from a faraway galaxy, though that could also be possible. To me, I see it as a kind, loving eye that emanates from one's family or community.

There seems to be an infinite number of patterns that repeat themselves from the tiniest of scales to the largest. If you ever had a chance to travel into outer space and see planet Earth shrinking into the size of a basketball, we humans would seem as tiny and trivial as free-floating cells, invisible to one's bare eyes. Yet this experience would not be self-deprecating nor demotivating, at least that's what astronauts told us. Samantha Cristoforetti, the first Italian woman to spend two hundred days in space, describes how her eyes were constantly 'saturated with sublime beauty, steeped in the splendor of the stars' and she felt this strong connection with humanity as a whole without losing her identity as an Italian. NASA astronaut Karen Nyberg felt a deep connection to the ecosystem on Earth while she was in orbit. She wrote for *National Geographic*:

> In the future, I would like to be more of an advocate for animal conservation. Every single part of the Earth reacts with every other part. It's one thing. Every little animal is important in that ecosystem. [Seeing the planet from above] makes you realize that, and makes you want to be a little more proactive in keeping it that way.[8]

---

[8] Nadia Drake, 'They Saw Earth From Space. Here's How It Changed Them', *National Geographic*, February 22, 2018, https://www.nationalgeographic.com/magazine/article/astronauts-space-earth-perspective.

When you get to see the cosmic perspective and realize that you're in fact part of something bigger, you start to realize that 'one small step of a man, [can potentially bring] one giant leap for mankind [and the whole world].' And you don't need to be Neil Armstrong to do that.

Imagine a frustrated child given the task of solving a complicated jigsaw puzzle. As he struggles to put those pieces together, almost in a state of despair, his good friend brings him the package box and shows him the end result—a beautiful picture or scenery of what it would turn out to be if only he continues at it. Now feeling inspired and reassured of an optimistic future, the boy returns to his task with new-found zest, hope, and meaning to carry on with his work. But the question is, where should he start? This wise friend then sits down with him and shares the hacks of becoming a dissectologist. They first sort the pieces of the jigsaw into groups based on the shapes, colours, and foreground images, then proceed to assemble the borders before assembling other parts that might share a similar pattern.

After spending hours and days working on this puzzling project, finally, they complete the jigsaw puzzle and take a step back to admire the fruit of their labour—a stunning piece of artwork. A sense of fulfilment springs from within. This child is in fact each and every one of us. We all need meaning, a compass, and sometimes a little help from a wise friend in life. Waking up to this cosmic perspective isn't what's most difficult. It is how our lives will change from now on, after having such an awakening, and what we will do for the rest of our lives.

The Dao of Flow is hopefully one such compass. It is a way of being that is in harmony with the rhythm or metapattern of nature. Those who follow this model will arrive at the same end goals despite taking different paths, for a metapattern manifests itself into an infinite number of patterns according to the disposition of each individual. For instance, the word 'harmony' connotes the meanings of 'ease, peace, moderation, order, agreement, and congruence', however, what is harmony for me may not necessarily be so for another person. Assuming that physical exercise brings harmony into one's lifestyle, the type and degree of exercise differ depending on each individual's body type and needs. For a professional athlete, working out takes up the bulk of their everyday life. For me, it's practising sixty minutes of yoga or taijiquan in the morning. For my brother, who works in a big corporation, it's playing badminton with his colleagues every weekend. For my late granny, harmony meant cultivating her garden every morning or simply taking a walk around the neighbourhood. Nonetheless, we all agree that moving our bodies makes us feel good. The means may vary, but the end goal is still to achieve harmony.

In this book, I hope to deconstruct some of the tenets, stages, and philosophy behind the Dao of Flow through stories and narratives I learned or encountered in my own life. These metapatterns are merely references to help you find your own unique dao of flow. As the great samurai philosopher Miyamoto Musashi wrote in *The Book of Five Rings*, 'if you know the Way broadly you will see it in all things.' This is an invitation to study the Way and practise it your way.

Author's artwork of a practising Aikido-ka

To focus on one thing yet able to 'transmute' (*hua* 化),
call it 'Numinous'.
To focus on one situation yet able to adapt and change,
call it 'Wisdom'.
—*Guanzi*

Chapter Three

流之道

The Three Esoteric Principles

'The supreme good is like regulating water.
Water benefits myriad things yet it is equanimous.
It dwells in places that people disdain.
Thus, it approximates the Dao.'

—*Laozi*[1]

The esoteric principles and practices behind the Dao of Flow stand as a core component to understanding the big picture of this book. In many ancient traditions, especially in Eastern contemplative discipline, something is 'esoteric' often not really because it is secretive, elite, superior, or dangerous; nor is it reserved to be fathomable only by a selected few saints or sages. Rather it is so because it requires back-and-forth interaction— oral or heart-to-heart transmission from a teacher based on their careful observation of the student's comprehension, execution,

---

[1] 「上善治（似）水。水善利萬物而有靜（爭），居眾之所惡，故幾於道矣。居善地，心善潚（淵），予善信，正（政）善治，事善能，動善時。夫唯不靜（爭），故無尤。」《长沙马王堆帛书老子甲乙本合订校订本》

and mastery of some form of art. Above all, it is usually experienced intuitively. I will try to distill the common essence from some of these practices in laymen's terms and provide a few simple exercises and examples that you can try to relate to your own life.

Taijiquan, aikido, Chinese calligraphy, yoga, tea, and Zen meditation as forms of contemplative practices that embody principles of the Dao were especially formative in shaping my psyche and were pivotal in developing the germinal ideas of this book. For the past decade, I've been practising on a daily basis the old-frame traditional Yang-style of taijiquan, an unbroken lineage that traces its roots to the eighteenth-century founding teacher, Yang Luchan. The main sequence consists of 108 forms or movements that are seamlessly connected in a series. Every single practice is an opportunity to clear one's mind and dwell on the sensations of one's movements. A full sequence takes, on average, twenty-five minutes to complete, but the sensitivity and mindfulness cultivated during this short period of time can permeate the rest of my day. Coming out from this moving meditation, interesting insights were sometimes discovered; habits gradually removed or formed, and it suddenly dawned on me one day that the esoteric principles of the Dao of Flow essentially boil down to mastering three things.

1. 松 (*song*)   The state of embodying water
2. 流 (*liu*)   The way of flowing water
3. 治 (*zhi*)   The art of regulating water

Embody. Flow. Regulate

Daoist philosophers and texts like *Laozi* and *Zhuangzi* have repeatedly used water as a metaphor to explain the unexplainable Dao. Even the most influential martial artist of the twentieth century, Bruce Lee, famously said: 'Empty your mind, be formless, shapeless—like water. Be water, my friend.'

But the real question is: How? How do we train ourselves to be like water?

Taijiquan offers one such methodology. Created by martial artists who tried to apply the principles of Dao, it is designed to systematically train and condition one's body and mind to reach a state akin to that of water. With more than hundred classic texts written, refined, and passed down from generation to generation over the past few centuries, taiji is an ancient art that can be practised physically, studied intellectually, and applied philosophically to all aspects of one's life. Like yoga, it begins with physical conditioning but ultimately extends into the spiritual domain.

To be like water, one must first understand the quality of water. In the *Daodejing*, water is said to resemble the supreme good because it nourishes all living beings effortlessly without conscious striving, and dwells in places that people disdain. Water transcends even the notion of duality. Like the symbol of yin and yang, it is nonchalantly traversing between states that only we humans perceive as high or low in an infinite number of cycles. Whilst we can only see rivers flowing from the top of a mountain down to the sea, what we don't visibly see is that at any point in time or stage of a flowing watercourse, some water is also evaporating and rising to the sky to form clouds that later return to earth as rainwater. Water, as the source of life, is ever-shifting and circulating.

In taiji, we're often reminded that the end goal of one's practice as well as one's life is to become like 'moving clouds and flowing water' (*xingyun liushui* 行雲流水)—a sense of stillness in motion that is natural and smooth without any sudden break or pause in between. Clouds and rivers move by submitting themselves completely to external forces. No matter how fast or slow a cloud may seem to be floating in the sky, it only moves according to the force of wind around it. Similarly, a river only flows downhill because it is driven by gravity. Its velocity is determined by factors such as the gradient of a slope, the shape and volume of a river, and the roughness of its riverbed. When a gradient or volume is higher, or when the friction is lower, water runs faster, and vice versa. But water does not resist change. It accepts any incoming condition, adapts accordingly, and moves on simply by taking up available space. Rivers and clouds share this common trait: they are completely fluid, soft, and yielding.

1. 松 The State of Embodying Water

'If one's form is not upright
Inner power will not come.
If one is not tranquil within
The heart will not be well-regulated
Align your form to uphold the inner power,
Emulate the humaneness of Heaven and rightfulness of earth
Then one's vitality is sustainable.'

—'Inward Training' chapter, *Guanzi*[2]

When applied to the human physical body, the first equivalent attribute of non-resistance is *song* 松・鬆 literally translated as 'loose' or 'relaxation'. However, I would further define *song* as **harmonious relaxation derived from cultivated wisdom and non-resistance**—an ability to tap into different modes of relaxation across the continuum, ranging from the complete letting go of one's body in sleep to varying degrees of physical and mental relaxation during one's wakefulness—depending on the activity. The real challenge is to intuitively know exactly where

---

[2] 「形不正，德不來。中不靜，心不治。正形攝德，天仁地義，則淫然而自至。」《管子・內業》

and how much one should relax in a given situation to achieve a state of harmony. To relax the body and mind at the right degree without slouching.

A mental experiment of *song* that I often engage in is to check in on my physical body when I'm doing my chores or out carrying my bag. While typing, reading, or walking, I ask myself, 'Are my shoulders tense or relaxed?' If my shoulders are slightly lifted, can I try and lower them down? Another tip is to pay careful attention, especially to the grip of one's hand. How strong are you holding on to the strap of your bag or your phone/wallet? And to what extent can you release the grip of your hand without dropping the items while walking? From what I observe, a lot of us unconsciously tense parts of our bodies (usually in the shoulders or neck) or overexert force (for example, in strongly grabbing something) while going around our daily chores on an autopilot mode. Why is that so?

Something is missing in our education. In modern culture, most people aren't taught about functional anatomy, kinaesthesia, or how to mindfully keep their bodies in a *song* 松 state. We're taught only to study, work, or push harder, and soon we begin to resist, not just mentally but also physically. Over time, we unconsciously develop certain mental habits and postures that are not conducive to our well-being—blockages in the physical and mental body. This is further exacerbated by a sedentary lifestyle and an onslaught of responsibility and burdens as we grow up. Embroiled in a hectic and stressful environment, many find their sympathetic nervous system over-activated, their breath fast-paced, short and shallow, and certain muscles disproportionately engaged, leading to formations of muscle knots and chronic discomfort. This crisis of not-knowing-how-to-relax is insidious and evident in the prevalence of insomnia that affects about 10 per cent to 35 per cent of our global population and in the escalation of depression, obesity, heart diseases, and various kinds of autoimmune disorders.[3] Our physical and mental well-being is being compromised as we deviate further and further away from this innate ability to relax—a skill and feeling we once knew intuitively as a child.

Most contemplative practices begin with de-conditioning negative habitual tendencies to restore a state of harmony and suppleness to our body, breath, and mind. In taijiquan and many other forms of martial arts, the foremost and fundamental training for beginners is 'standing-stake' (*zhanzhuang* 站樁) a few stances that you hold statically to learn your body's alignment and to develop a strong yet relaxed structure (*song* 松).

---

[3] 'Insomnia Awareness Day facts and stats', American Academy of Sleep Medicine, https://sleepeducation.org/insomnia-awareness-day-facts-stats/.

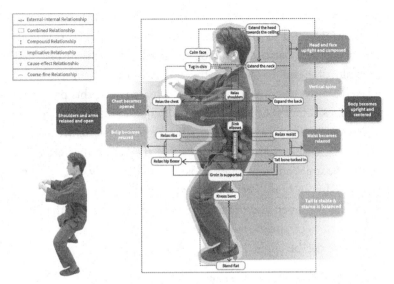

An infographic explaining the body alignment of standing like
a tree, an exercise that anyone can perform at home.
Photos taken by Arjun Sai Krishnan.

Note that the polysemous character 松 *song* has multiple nuances. It
also means 'pine tree'—an evergreen conifer plant genus known as
matsu in Japan and *sonamu* in Korea—that is much loved and grown
across East Asia. Pines are a popular motif in poetry and ink wash
painting because of their elegance and pleasing aesthetic. They are
lauded for being highly adaptive to different geographical climates,
seasons, and temperature changes, and are among the few types of
trees that can remain lush and green throughout winter. Flexible
and bendy in nature, certain species can be pruned and trained to
make particularly good bonsai specimens, while out in the wild,
pines usually stand out among the tallest and strongest trees that
can live up to hundreds and even thousands of years. Altogether,
pine trees symbolize hope, resilience, longevity, and steadfastness.

I believe there's a correlation between the relaxed state of
song 松 and the characteristics of pine trees. In *zhanzhuang*, we're
essentially standing like a tree or a 'stake'—solid wood or metal post
that is driven into the ground to support a plant or a fence. Just as a
strong pine tree is undeterred by winds and storms by extending its

root systems deep into the ground to support its height, *zhanzhuang* is the foundation to strengthen all the core muscles in our body that bolster our balance and stability while keeping the rest relaxed. Mentally, it helps to develop the fortitude of staying calm and relaxed amidst discomfort. In Japanese martial arts, this practice is sometimes referred to as *kibadachi* 騎馬立ち or 'horse stance' and is practised in the school of aikido that I was trained in. My teacher, Seiko Ito sensei, used to remind us that the key to mastering *aiki* 合気 (the unification of one's *qi*) is to 'feel the *omosa* 重さ (weight) of water' in our body. Feel the sinking of fluid to the centre of your body, the abdomen and the lower halves of your body—the lower portion of feet, quads, glutes, naval, arms, forearms, and fingers. The same can be applied to yoga poses.

Relax the shoulders.
Stay grounded.
Lengthen the breath.
Soften the gaze.
Compose yourself.

Left: Master Chan assisting the author to align his
form to approximate *song* 松.
Right: A *song* 松 pine tree painting by Chinese artist Cui Wenhuan.

After a few minutes in *zhanzhuang*, one's leg muscles may become sore, and the heart and breath will soon race faster, but still, we're encouraged to hold on just a little longer. To an external observer, one may seem quietly engaged in a yin form of practice, but internally, the practitioner is actually building up a reservoir of scorching hot yang energy. If during *zhanzhuang* one can remain upright yet relaxed, and maintain this sensation of sunken water in the body and mind for an extended period of time, then they can easily do it elsewhere. The real challenge lies in staying *song* 松 throughout the day, in what Zen masters sometimes say *xingzhu zuowo* 行住坐臥:

行 (*xing*): walking
住 (*zhu*): standing
坐 (*zuo*): sitting
臥 (*wo*): lying down

Like our physical body, the mental state of *song* 松 can be explained in terms of water. In one of Van Gogh's letters to his brother Theo, the Dutch painter wrote, 'The heart of man is very much like the sea, it has its storms, it has its tides and in its depths, it has its pearls too.' Whether in *zhanzhuang* or any form of meditation, one easily finds oneself swept away in an ocean of thoughts like waves oscillating on the surface of a sea. Our goal is not to swim against the waves nor forcefully stop them but to embrace all of them in their totality. Because when we fully embody the mind like water, we can find stillness everywhere—amidst the roaring storm, along a flowing river, and on a quiet lake. No single wave, no ephemeral thought nor emotion can perturb you. You are both a tiny drop of water as well as the vast blue ocean itself. Ironically, by fully embodying water and letting go of resistance in our mind, it will flow naturally and settle down on its own, when all of a sudden, we find ourselves disappearing into the depths of an ocean, entering into a state of deep relaxation yet heightened clarity—the mental equivalent of *song* 松. This relates to the Daoist concept of 'effortless action' (*wuwei* 無為)—to achieve something without intentional forcing. The goal of meditation, Dao-istically speaking, is to stop the waves without stopping the waves.

No matter what activity we're engaged in, whether it's walking along the streets, having a meeting, working out in the gym, or reading this book right now, we can check in on ourselves and see if there's any unnecessary tension physically or mentally. If physical, relax simply by feeling the weight of water in that region of one's body. Let it settle down. Mentally, *song* 松 is neither being lethargic nor hyper-focused, but rather implies sustaining a gentle yet mindful awareness of the present moment. On the physical level, it is to neither slouch nor over-engage our body, but to keep a balanced and healthy shape or posture that is harmonious and elegant, like a pine tree.

2. 流 The Way of Flowing Water

After feeling, quietening, and embodying the water within, we can now proceed from static holding to dynamic moving. Here, one learns how to flow and move water while still maintaining a state of *song* 松. When the body and mind are one like water, they can move easily and gracefully according to your intent without any obstruction, like clouds and rivers flowing in accordance with the force of wind and gravity. However, our body and mind do require some training.

When something flows, there's a constant change of yin and yang. For example, when you pour water from a filled cup into an empty cup. The latter cup changes from a state of emptiness (*xu* 虛) to fullness (*shi* 實), and the former cup the other way round. Daoist artists and scientists study, analyse, and fine-tune yin-yang changes in every phenomenon to facilitate a smooth, natural, and harmonious transition between the two polarities.

In taiji, the act of leaning your weight over to your right foot makes it 'full' (*shi* 實) and heavy, while the left foot, which becomes light and weightless is more 'empty' (*xu* 虛). Same with walking, fullness and emptiness are constantly flowing from one to another between our two moving legs. If you lift or kick with the left leg, this action of attacking now becomes aggressive yang, while if you're only raising the leg to defend against an attack, then it can also be interpreted as defensive yin. Yin-yang exists in every phenomenon and change according to circumstances, but as a general rule of thumb, yang is usually associated with pushing, opening, exerting force, and exhalation; yin with pulling, closing, releasing force, and inhalation.

A trained practitioner is aware of the subtle nuances of yin and yang interchanging in their environment, body, movement, breath, and intention. This is the reason why taiji is usually practised in slow motion at the outset. As a matter of fact, when I first started learning, my teacher personally supervised that I practise at a constant velocity and as slow as I could possibly go. If I were to start lifting my arms at a speed of 5 inches per second at the very beginning, ideally, I would have to maintain this pace throughout the whole sequence, as well as to keep a more or less consistent height. Healthy and younger students are encouraged to keep a lower stance throughout the whole practice, toning their glutes and quads, while older participants can squat at a higher degree comfortable to their own joint mobility and endurance.

There are several reasons for being low, slow, and uniform. One is that time feels dilated, and it helps practitioners develop a high level of sensitivity towards their bodily sensations, yin-yang transitions, breath coordination while still maintaining an upright yet relaxed posture—*song*. In fact, we're allowed to move fast, but only if we can keep the same level of alignment and awareness in check. Secondly, moving slowly helps activate the parasympathetic nervous system and calms down the monkey mind—just like walking meditation. We're cultivating the quality of inner stillness (yin) flowing amidst external movements (yang). Finally, it offers an experiential gateway to learn an important principle in taiji: the optimization of efficiency within a harmonious self-sustaining system.

In other words, we're trying to use the least amount of resources or minimal effort in maximizing the output, which in this case means moving naturally without exerting unnecessary force on the body.

This third reason can be explained in terms of physics and relates to why we initially learn to move at a consistent velocity. The goal is to train ourselves to approximate an 'ideal mechanism'—a hypothetical device capable of transmitting power without adding to or subtracting from it. In an ideal machine, 'energy and power are not lost or dissipated through friction, deformation, wear, or other inefficiencies,' thus ensuring optimal performance and preventing wear and tear. When moving at a consistent speed without any abrupt acceleration or deceleration, only a minimal force is applied in overcoming resistance, so the net force of motion is kept close to zero. Recall our high school physics equation:

$F = MA$
Force = Mass x Acceleration
If acceleration is zero, the net force is zero.

Perhaps the best explanation is through the analogy of driving a car. Hypothetically speaking, the most efficient way of driving is to drive using only the accelerator and using the braking pedal at its minimum. Imagine driving alone in a circular circuit arena. You press on the accelerator to reach a speed of 100 kilometres per hour. Maintain this velocity for some time, then take your foot off the pedal and allow the car to slow down on its own. Theoretically, you have just maximized the total distance travelled using the tiniest amount of fuel, applying no self-imposed resistance throughout the journey and braking only once at the very end. This scenario is of course impossible in the real world of driving when you need to slow down before traffic lights, stop at various turns, and adapt to other erratic drivers around you to avoid a collision. However, once we understand this vision of an 'ideal harmonious form of maximizing efficiency' and internalize this principle into our body and mind, we return to the real world with a different paradigm.

I started noticing changes in my behaviour, especially in driving. When I get into the car, instead of hurling myself onto the seat, I enter softly. I take an upright yet relaxed sitting posture without gripping too hard on the steering wheel. Overall, I try to maintain a calm and comfortable speed that would enable me to arrive at my destination in time without any sudden jerks of acceleration or deceleration, much like doing taiji. Not only does it help save petrol in my tank, but also more of my mental reserve. Just like the cup-pouring analogy, you can pour water slowly from one to another, ensuring a smooth flow of water; or you could do it recklessly, splashing water everywhere and wasting your reserve. No objections to those who can execute it quickly if they can do it in a smooth, precise, and efficient manner. As long as the means and outcome are harmonious, speed can be relative.

The principle of maximizing output with minimum input is often expressed in the famous taijiquan saying:

'With the right influence or skilful means, four ounces can move a thousand pounds.' (*qiandong siliang boqianjin* 牽動四兩撥千斤)

The phrase 'skilful means' is key here. You cannot move a thousand pounds with brute force. Only with the force of wisdom, the force of *song* 松. This principle is best illustrated by an equestrian who is able to ride a thousand-pound horse gracefully by controlling its direction, gait, and speed with minimum effort, using just his legs, cues, and rein. When walking, trotting, cantering, or galloping, the rider's body would move in tandem with the rhythm of the horse, as if they had merged into one, and the horse would obediently follow his intent without any resistance. The Taijiquan Classics proceed to explain that in order to move a thousand pounds with four ounces, you'll need to learn how to 'stick and continuously follow' (*zhanlian niansui* 沾連黏隨)[4] your opponent's movements and gain an advantageous position over them. Similarly, if riders move in a strange and uncoordinated way, horses get annoyed and confused—as often as not disobeying them.

Shi 勢

This scenario implicates a couple of things. In any case, whether it's solving a problem, completing a task, or trying to learn something, there is always an opportune moment, a skilful means, or an optimized physical and mental state that one can find or tap into that will lead to the maximization of one's output. In Chinese philosophy, this is called *shi* 勢—what French sinologist Jean Francois would translate as, 'the propensity of things'. In *Sun Tzu: The Art of War*, Roger Ames calls it 'strategic advantage':

> 'That the velocity of cascading water can send boulders bobbing about is due to its strategic advantage (*shi* 勢). That a bird of prey when it strikes can smash its victim to pieces is due to its timing. So, it is with the expert at battle that his strategic advantage is channelled and his timing is precise. His strategic advantage is like a drawn crossbow and his timing is like releasing the trigger.' (Ames, 1993, p. 87).

Shi not only applies to taiji or driving but to other areas of one's life. However, it requires cultivation and refinement to become effortless, and the wisdom to know when, where, and how. Upon mastery, the means and results are often felt and described as 'flow'. What was once difficult and challenging can now be achieved with ease, grace, and harmony after you've succeeded

---

[4] Full poem:「掤捋擠按須認真， 上下相隨人難進。任他巨力來打我，牽動四兩撥千斤。引進落空合即出， 沾連黏隨不丟頂。」王宗岳《太極拳論‧打手歌》

in perfecting the skills. At this point, everything seems to happen on its own, like 'moving clouds and flowing water' (*xingyun liushui* 行雲流水).

Similar training of maximizing efficiency through inner flow is found in ancient Japanese wisdom, especially in the art of swordsmanship and aikido. In fact, the Japanese katana itself was initially designed to optimize lethality. Engineered by highly accomplished craftsmen using tamahagane—a kind of specialized Japanese steel smelted with varying layers of carbon concentration—katanas are beautifully designed as mildly-curved single-edged swords, strong enough to deliver both powerful cuts and thrusts with minimum force. Samurai and *kenjutsuka* (practitioners of swordsmanship) are often caught up in the practise of *suburi* 素振り, the swinging of their katana up and down hundreds of times, a seemingly mundane and ineffectual activity. What's the point of repeating the same simple movement again and again after knowing how to do it?

Author practising suburi under the guidance of Seiko Ito sensei

The real purpose of this practice isn't just weight-training or merely learning how to slash, but rather to condition oneself to *maintain a specific state of being when slashing.* This meditative state of being, equivalent to *song* is sometimes referred to in budo as *zanshin* 残心), a remaining or lingering mind. *Zanshin* is a state of relaxed alertness that one should maintain before, during, and after an action has been performed because a samurai must always be prepared for any preemptive attack. Besides cultivating unflinching precision, suburi is practised to unite one's subconscious body and mind to move fluidly and gently as a connected whole, utilizing only the minimum yet most powerful force in wielding a sword. Ideally, one should keep the shoulders down and relaxed, initiating movements not from the arms but from the core of the body—the *tanden* (Chinese: *dantian* 丹田). He lifts the sword handle up to a point just slightly higher than the forehead, feels the force of gravity, and yields to it by allowing the edge of the katana to slice forward and down in a nice rounded curvature. When examined closely, the grip on the katana is as soft and gentle as if one is holding on to the limbs of a baby. 'Let go not of the force, but of the force that does not serve you.'[5] Seiko Ito sensei would often remind us.

Embodiment of Song 松 *in Flow*

This 'gentle yet firm grip or touch' is an extension of *song* 松 in action. It holds the secret to mastering aikido and taijiquan—in sensing, holding, grappling, toppling, or throwing one's opponent. Our hands, especially the fingertips are one of the most touch-sensitive parts of the human body. They contain thousands of sensory receptors and a high density of specialized nerve endings that are constantly communicating with our brain in receiving and analyzing information, as well as in initiating responses. Human emotions are more often than not directly reflected in the state of our hands. Sincerity and confidence can be felt in a genuine handshake. Intimacy is transmitted through a warm touch. When

---

[5] 「力が抜けるじゃなくて、意識的に無駄な力を抜くことです。」

people are angry, they tend to clench their fists tight; when nervous or fearful, our hands sweat or tremble. We even create stimuli for happiness and connection through the act of clapping or patting someone's shoulder.

In a publication titled 'Evolution der Hand', Putz and Tuppek wrote:

> The more recent evolution of the hand can be understood as the expression of the development of the brain . . . it is a direct tool of our consciousness, a main source of differentiated tactile sensations as well as a precise working organ . . . [and] direct expressions of our personality.

If calf muscles are regarded as the secondary heart of the circulatory system, perhaps our hands can be considered as a secondary cerebrum in the nervous system, or as Kant suggests, 'an extension of our human brain.

Thus, by mastering the state of our hands, we can almost directly influence our emotions and psyche. A well-conditioned, firm yet gentle tactile response can automatically prime one's body and consciousness into a state of flow. While writing, by learning how to soften the grip on my brush or pen, I realized this awareness naturally extends to the softening of my gaze, the straightening of my posture, and the relaxation of my arms and shoulders. This creates a conducive holistic state of being for longer hours of writing without getting tired. The same applies to driving, walking, or doing any other activity. Zen teaching intimates that we can learn a lot about ourselves and our deepest subjective habits and patterns from the way we go around our daily chores. A person with an untrained coarse mind tends to gobble up food, speak excessively, or brush the floor in an agitated rough manner; a cultivated subtle mind consumes food gracefully, speaks mindfully, and gently sweeps the floor in a methodical yet effective fashion. Ideally, the state of *song* or *zanshin* should be trained regularly and infused into one's daily life.

In essence, flow is the state of *song* and non-resistance in one's thoughts and actions—a beautiful balance between yin and yang; softness and strength; focus and relaxation that will yield maximum productivity without violent brute force.

3. 治 The Art of Regulating Water

The third esoteric principle takes into account the regulation of water within the grand scheme of things. In other words, it is integration, which involves the graceful transitions between yin and yang; stillness and flow that leads to a beautiful end result that is balanced and harmonious. At any point, if required, one may temporarily move towards some form of extreme but ultimately contributes to a harmonious end goal. When the work is finalized, there are two important criteria that indicate a harmonized and regulated flow: *le* 樂 and *yun* 韻

Le 樂

樂 means joy or pleasure when pronounced as *le*; but when pronounced as *yue* it also means music or, more accurately speaking, the Greek-Latin word *harmonia*—agreement, concord of sounds—that we've introduced in the earlier chapter. There is of course an etymological relationship between the two definitions. The agreement, concord of sounds naturally give rise to feelings of joy in the listener and the performer, as well as help to harmonize relationships between different classes and groups of people. Perhaps this is why many ancient sages such as Confucius encouraged commoners to pick up musical instruments such as the Guqin as a form of self-development. As written in the Record of Music chapter of *The Book of Rites*:

> All sound is born in the heart. *Yue* or harmonious music is coherent with *li*—the proper conduct and principles of this universe. Animals can perceive sound, but not its modulations; Most people can perceive modulations, but not necessarily

the *harmonia* of *yue*. Only the wise can perceive *yue*. On this account, one can potentially discriminate voice in order to know the sounds; the sounds in order to know the harmonious music of *yue*, and the harmonious music in order to know the right virtue of good governance and the Dao of Order . . . Thus the understanding of *yue* brings one closer to understanding 'order' *li*. One who has mastered both *li* and *yue* can be pronounced as a virtuous person.[6]

Of course, music as one of the earliest forms of flow-inducing entertainment born out of ritual is only one means through which we can pierce into the order or metapatterns of life and the cosmological manifestation of nature. Similar patterns are found across other contemplative practices, sports, arts, and potentially in everything we do in life. The feeling of joy and concord *le* 樂 is not confined to music if one can master flow harmoniously. Hungarian-American psychologist Mihaly Csikszentmihalyi, in his seminal work *Flow: The Psychology of Optimal Experience* wrote:

> The happiest people spend much time in a state of flow – the state in which people are so involved in an activity that nothing else seems to matter; the experience itself is so enjoyable that people will do it even at great cost, for the sheer sake of doing it.[7]

Just as the concordance of rhythm and melody brings joy to the listener, the congruence of one's body, mind, and spirit in an

---

[6] 「凡音者， 生於人心者也。樂者， 通倫理者也。是故知聲而不知音者， 禽獸是也；知音而不知樂者， 眾庶是也。唯君子為能知樂。是故審聲以知音， 審音以知樂， 審樂以知政， 而治道備矣。是故不知聲者不可與言音， 不知音者不可與言樂。知樂則幾於禮矣。禮樂皆得， 謂之有德。德者得也。」《禮記‧樂記》

[7] Mihaly Csikszentmihalyi, *Flow: The Psychology of Optimal Experience* (New York: Harper & Row, 1990), p. 4.

activity naturally leads to a sense of peace and happiness to the 'flow-er'.

Yun 韻

Esoterically speaking, a second criterion of well-regulated flow is *yun* 韻, which I think is one of the most difficult Chinese characters to be translated into other languages. Yet, the comprehension of its true meaning can reveal something invaluable about the ideal goal of East Asian aesthetics and philosophy. Commonly translated as 'rhyme or sweet music', the ancient dictionary of *Shuowen Jiezi* says that '*yun* is harmony' (韻: 和也) . So, what is lost in translation? In my opinion, *yun* 韻 can be defined as a lingering joyful sensation, a pleasant aftertaste or strong impression that flows deep into one's consciousness and remains there due to the effect of experiencing something uniquely harmonious.

The experience is pleasant and joyful so much so that one longs to relive that experience.

Take note of the word 'uniquely' harmonious. *Yun* 韻 necessitates a sort of distinctive feature and differentiated qualities that makes it unique, yet the overall picture is harmonious. It is built on the foundation of deep work and increasing complexity. Take Pablo Picasso for example. His artwork is derived from the mastery and combination of different styles, techniques, as well as his own self-developed form of 'Cubism', which often appeared childlike, abstracted, and sometimes fragmented like a broken mirror. Yet there's both a sense of harmony and uniqueness that is captivating and beautiful. This is Picasso's *yun* 韻, if you may. Most first-rate artists have their own definitive *yun* 韻. You find a common thread, a distinctive quality in their masterpiece artworks.

If you're familiar with Chinese culture, you may have heard of the term *yun* 韻 sometimes being used in combination with other characters. For instance, *fengyun* 風韻 is often used to describe the graceful appeal of a lady who is characterized by beauty and elegance, such that she leaves a lasting impression in one's head. Musicologists speak of *qinyun* 琴韻—the lingering of musical rhythm or melody in one's head after a superb performance of the Chinese zither. *Qinyun* is the combined product of one's mastery over a musical piece and the infusion of an individual player's unique feelings and expression within the music. Without the player's feelings and unique expression, it would only sound robotic and trite.

Tea connoisseurs are always searching for specific kinds of *chayun* 茶韻 that defines say a good green tea, oolong tea, or Pu'er tea. Depending on its origin, fermentation process, and method of making tea, these teas would deliver very disparate kinds of *chayun*. For example, one of the most famous kinds of oolong tea is Wuyi tea, which is prized for its distinctive terroir called *yanyun* 岩韻 (terroir of mineral rocks) that results from being cultivated in Fujian's Wuyi mountains. Today you may find Wuyi tea in many shops around the world, which may taste like oolong tea but lacks the terroir or *yanyun*. The same can be said with Pu'er Tea, which we will touch in a later chapter. *Yun* is also sometimes elaborated as *shenyun* 神韻 (神 meaning divine, soul, spirit, or nature). Another important compound word shared in both Chinese and Japanese is *yuyun·yoin* (餘韻・余韻)—a harmonious aftertaste, reverberation, or legacy that remains. Thus, the consummation of *yun* is something that feels elegant, spiritual, long-lasting, and most importantly, natural. It is also the harmonizing deeds that stay on in the memories of others long after one is gone. Heaven and Human becoming One, essentially (*tianren heyi* 天人合一).

Let's return to 'Yu's Taming of the Flood' for a minute to delineate the three esoteric principles. In Yu's rudimentary efforts of understanding water, he figured out that: 1) it will either continuously flow downwards, or 2) settle down in collected bodies of water in inland ponds and lakes or coastal seas. This complies with the first esoteric principle of embodying water instead of resisting it. He then proceeded to master the second esoteric principle of learning how to flow water (literally!) through digging canals and building irrigation systems. But flow itself would not suffice if he was diverting water out of only one segment of the Yellow River, or within the scope of one province. Yu had to bring to completion the third esoteric principle of regulating or harmonizing flow by analysing China's map and determining various locations where channeling of water is required. The solution to such a huge crisis lies in big picture thinking, to see the forest for the trees. This final principle ensures that no single village is flooded or undersupplied with water and maximizes overall work efficiency.

In movement-based contemplative practices such as taiji or yoga, we first learn to embody the different shapes of our body such as in *zhanzhuang* or *asanas*—static poses. Then we learn to flow our body by stringing different poses together into a sequence or *vinyasa* in coordination with one's breath and movement. Finally, one has to consider the effect of flow in relation to a bigger picture. This bigger picture could mean the general harmony of flow from the very beginning of a sequence to its end. For example, in yoga, a good sequence usually begins with the warming up of one's body, strengthening and stretching from the periphery—our exterior joints, limbs, hips, and shoulders—towards the mobility of our central spine, and then ending with an inversion and savasana to bring a sense of balance and peace to the very end of the yoga class. In a larger context, this bigger picture can refer to the harmony of one's life. How does yoga, a routine, an activity, or an endeavour fit harmoniously into your lifestyle, family, community, or higher purpose?

Traditional Chinese Medicine and Myofascia Continuities

We find these three esoteric principles recurring across different fields and domains especially in the mastery of eastern arts and sciences. One interesting example is Traditional Chinese Medicine (TCM). In the book *Metapatterns*, biologist Tyler Volk wrote: 'The flows of vital fluids within tubes in similar-looking networks—rivers, plants, blood systems—can lead to a view of Earth itself as an organism.' The converse is also true. TCM views the human body as an ecosystem—one in which meridians, fascia, nerves, and blood vessels are all interconnected like a complex river system. When a blockage occurs, it may result in sudden outbursts of resources or a lack of supply to certain parts of the body—disrupting harmony and causing diseases. The solution lies in 'flow' or so-called 'channel theory'. The Yuan medical scientist Zhi Zhenheng summarized: 'When *qi* and blood are flowing in harmony, sickness shall not arise.' (氣血沖和，萬病不生)

Recent studies in Western anatomy are now suggesting a similar approach to manual therapy, as well as a potential connection between the channel theory of Chinese medicine and the fascial network of the human body. Anatomist and writer Tom Myers, through his decades of research in dissection, clinical application, and movement studies, has developed and put forward a set of twelve specific fascial lines in the body that transmit pull, strain, and rebound across 'myofascia'—'the bundled together inseparable nature of muscle tissue (myo-) and its accompanying web of connective tissue (fascia).'

Fascia can be seen as a kind of gel-like sticky yet greasy fabric that wraps around our whole body, holding everything firmly in place and constantly adjusting and building up new layers of fibers to accommodate the needs of our body. Together, the fascial lines work as one integrated system that facilitates movement and supports the stability of our physical structure. However, a bad posture, an injury, or any imbalance along one line could over a period of time lead to pain and dysfunction elsewhere in the body. An unresolved strain in the plantar fascia of one's foot could potentially lead to discomfort in the knees and unhealthy compensation in the hips and lower back. In an article for the Yoga Journal, Myers wrote:

> Tension in your body—slumping your shoulders forward, for example—prompts the fibroblasts to make more fibers that will arrange themselves along the line of stress. These bulked-up fascial fibers will form a barrier that will slow or stop capillary-sourced food from reaching your cells. You'll get enough to survive, but function will slow down. In addition to a thicker barrier of fascial-tissue fibers, the mucus that completes your fluid fascial network will also become thicker and more turgid, which contributes to stopping the flow to your cells.[8]

This reinforces the importance of maintaining a *song* 松 and healthy posture in our day-to-day living. On the other hand, a hands-on approach called Myofascia Release Techniques (MFR) to stretch, knead, and work out these 'bulked-up fascial fibers' a.k.a knots or trigger points in the body is now gaining attention and popularity worldwide. MFR can be done by a trained manual therapist using one's hands, elbows, or tools such as massage guns, balls, and foam rollers. An incisive structural integrator can accurately assess his or her patient's overall postural pattern and develop treatment strategies to unwind and resolve unhealthy compensations, either through the strengthening of weak connective tissues or the loosening of tight regions. After breaking down those fascia knots, it is imperative to decondition negative postural habits and start cultivating healthy ones. That is why MFR is sometimes coupled with physiotherapy or movement-based practices such as yoga and qigong to strengthen, stretch, and restore the balance of myofascia continuities. When skilful pressure is applied to

---

[8] Tom Myers, 'What You Need to Know About Fascia', *Yoga Journal*, January 18, 2018, https://www.yogajournal.com/teach/anatomy-yoga-practice/what-you-need-to-know-about-fascia-2/.

the fascia, they also become hydrated and more permeable, thus facilitating the flow of molecules through the fibrous web to improve overall circulation in the body.

Like rivers sustaining rich biodiversity of flora and fauna along their paths, *qi* and blood flow throughout the body to nourish our organs, tissues, and cells. Therefore, the Daoist approach to healing lies in using all kinds of skilful means to remove blockages, prevent stagnation, and cultivate a harmonious circulation of *qi* and blood within the body. This may include the consumption of healthy food or medicine, triggering meridian points with moxibustion and needles, bodywork massage, or moving one's body through practices such as qigong or taijiquan. Even though Chinese medicine cannot prevent or cure all diseases, many concepts and practices from Chinese medicine can contribute to the body's overall health in a holistic way. The secret to health and longevity is summarized in one of Qibo's expositions in the *Yellow Emperor's Classic of Medicine*:

> The ancient sages who understood the Dao knew how to regulate yin and yang, and harmonize various skills and calculations. They kept a moderate diet, cultivated healthy lifestyle habits, and toiled without wasting their mental reserve. Thus, their physical form and spirit were both fully equipped, and they were able to max out their life expectancy, passing away beyond centenarians.[9]

Today, the 'pop a pill' mentality is becoming outdated. More people are becoming aware of the need for holistic healing, and the Dao of Flow is making its mark in the field of health and wellness.

---

[9] 「歧伯對曰：上古之人，其知道者，法於陰陽，和於術數，食飲有節，起居有常，不妄作勞，故能形與神俱，而盡終其天年，度百歲乃去。」《黃帝內經・素問・上古天真論》

Daoist Alchemy

'A wizard's power of Changing and of Summoning can shake
the balance of the world. It is dangerous, that power. It is most
perilous. It must follow knowledge, and serve need. To light a
candle is to cast a shadow . . .'

—Ursula K. Leguin in *A Wizard of Earthsea*

Thus, a true Daoist alchemist can discern the internal and
external polarity of a given entity at any given time and catalyze,
complement, or transform yin and yang correspondingly to
achieve a state of harmony.

This is evident in a highly skilled doctor who knows how to
prescribe the right medicine to restore health, in a physical trainer
or bodywork therapist who understands the mechanics of the
human body, knowing which connective tissues to strengthen or
stretch to keep one's body in balance; in an emotionally intelligent
leader who intuitively makes everyone in the room feel at home;
in an entrepreneur who sees a business opportunity to solve a
societal problem; in a teacher who understands the psychology
of learning so profoundly that they are adept in using various
pedagogical tools to ignite curiosity—even among those students
who seem most apathetic. And sometimes, if we're lucky, we find
a political leader who knows the Way to heal and transform chaos
and suffering towards peace and harmony.

While we begin the three esoteric principles from the
perspective of Yu the Great, contemplative practices, and
optimal health, I hope to demonstrate in later chapters that the
embodiment, flow, and regulation of water can be found in other
individuals in specific domains and social influences. Now, I invite
you to wander alongside me on a personal odyssey.

Author practising Taijiquan on Joshoji temple ground in Japan.
Photo taken by Gabriel Ng.

Part II

Yun 雲

Wandering Cloud

行 雲 流 水

Chapter Four

絆

Kizuna: My Journey to Japan

Reflecting on the flow of my life, I was surprised to discover several 'turning points' that were potentially characterized in Chinese terminology as *shi* 勢. Like cascading water sending boulders bobbing down a stream, *shi* is a pivotal moment, a force in life that propelled me forward into the unknown future, yet looking back, it was the knot that tied everything together. A *shi* for instance—generated more than a century ago—was when my great grandparents left Shantou, China, on a steamboat to Penang and settled down in Malaysia. Today we preserve much of our native dialects, cultural arts, and rituals, yet in a country that is a 'cultural melting pot', I have also simultaneously become receptive towards other beliefs and accustomed to thinking and speaking in several languages—Minnan dialect, English, Mandarin, and Malay. Here in Southeast Asia, I found myself growing up on a bridge intersecting East and West—a strategic advantage that provided me with a unique and humbling perspective of seeing the world.

The most pivotal *shi* in my life came about in 2013, when I joined a humanitarian trip to Fukushima and volunteered at a nuclear refugee centre for senior citizens. It was the last year of my high school and I was facing my end-of-adolescence crisis. I had no idea what I wanted to study nor where I should apply for university. The situation was further aggravated by my father's failing business, which was on the verge of bankruptcy. All I knew was that I really wanted to get out of my home country and study abroad elsewhere, and I needed financial support. A senior friend of mine, Jyon, handed me a pamphlet of a week-long international youth exchange programme in Japan and encouraged me to join. The title of this exchange programme was 'Crisis Management'— How did Japan cope with this natural disaster? What can we do to mitigate or prevent similar crises in the future? And how can we apply what we learned from Japan in our own life?

'Who knows, you might discover something about yourself from this programme,' Jyon said. He was affiliated with the organizing team and said he could get me on the programme for free, but I would need to finance my own travelling expenses. I sought out a local business networking group and pitched for a round-trip ticket to Japan with the promise that I would present my learnings to them when I returned. The funding was approved.

Author standing on the remains of a cemetery next to the surviving temple in Iwaki.

A few months later, I found myself standing on the shore of Iwaki in Fukushima. Smelling the salty scent of seawater from the warm summer breeze, I took off my shoes on the white sandy beach and slowly paced towards the open sea. There was nothing around us but an old Zen temple on the right with a cemetery in its backyard. The vast blue Pacific Ocean was surprisingly calm and peaceful that day, but behind those murmuring sea waves, one could hear the cry of pain and sadness. With my palms folded in *gassho*, I whispered a few words of prayer, 'May all suffering ones be suffering-free.'

The disturbing footage of a thirty-metre high tsunami engulfing the coastline city returned to me. Triggered by a 9.0 magnitude earthquake, huge tidal waves came crashing into the shore of Tōhoku, Japan, on 11 March 2011—toppling buildings, uprooting trees, and sweeping away innocent civilians. It was all on TV, which felt unreal back then, but now being here myself and listening to stories shared by survivors, I was personally confronted with a past reality that was once so distanced away. Thousands had perished where I stood, hundreds of thousands of people were displaced, and the aftermath was further exacerbated by a nuclear meltdown at the Fukushima Daiichi Nuclear Power Plant. Japan was facing, and is still facing, one of the worst crises ever. In the face of a life-or-death situation, one's personal problems seemed trivial. I had a glimpse into the impermanence of our existence as I contemplated how death can come at any time.

I was reminded of a dystopian short story called 'The Ones Who Walk Away from Omelas' by Ursula K. Le Guin. The story suggests that the joy and happiness of people in Omelas, a fictitious city, are paid in the form of dark injustice and pain that has befallen a strange child locked in perpetual filth, darkness, and misery. Everyone in Omelas knows about the child's existence, most people have even seen this child.

But they choose to turn a blind eye, returning to their day-to-day living. Occasionally, someone having seen the child, chooses not to go home, but instead walks straight out of the city towards the mountains, never to return.

> The city of happiness, well, we all live there and people go
> about their business with full knowledge of the child in the
> closet . . . They all know that it has to be there . . . they all
> understand that their happiness, the beauty of their city . . .
> depend(s) wholly on this child's abominable misery.[10]

The message that I brought away from Fukushima is that we're not going to walk away from Omelas nor are we going to live our happy lives while turning a blind eye to the sufferings of others. True compassion demands action. This was evident in the efforts of countless volunteers who flew in from across Japan to help and support those affected by the disasters, and especially in the noble work of individuals like Koyu Abe.

Koyu Abe: A Zen Priest's Effort to Decontaminate Fukushima

When I first met Koyu Abe, he was just like any other Zen priest, well-dressed in dark blue robes with a clean-shaven head. He had some sort of a solemn-looking straight-face, but when our eyes met, and I tried to say *konnichiwa*, the Zen-looking face melted into an awkward smile, followed by an attempt to start a conversation. But since I couldn't understand Japanese at that time, and he spoke little English, we ended up just nodding and giggling. I later found out that he was actually one of our workshop speakers.

---

[10] Le Guin, Ursula K, 'The Ones Who Walk Away from Omelas: A Story.' Wind's Twelve Quarters Story, (New York: Harper Perennial, 2017).

Koyu Abe explaining about his work on decontaminating
Fukushima to students from various countries. Author in
grey hoodie sitting in the front row.

Since 2011, Abe has been working arduously to help revitalize
Fukushima. As the chief priest of Joenji Temple, he has provided
emotional support and solace to the local people by offering
prayers and burial services for thousands left dead or missing from
the earthquake and tsunami. He has also cultivated and distributed
hundreds of thousands of sunflowers and seeds around Fukushima,
hoping to help absorb radiation from the soil and to cheer up
the local residents. Sunflowers were said to be useful after the
Chernobyl nuclear disaster in absorbing Iodine and Cesium from
the soil through their roots, which could, later on, be disposed
of as 'hyper-accumulators'. This helped to trap and concentrate
radiation particles in a targeted area that would otherwise seep
into the ground and spread. In addition to that, Koyu Abe has also
gathered volunteers and initiated a grassroots movement to track
down and clean up radioactive 'hot spots' around the city. Armed
with Geiger counters, they would go around the city every day,

detecting any irregular spikes of radiation, and upon discovering one, spend several hours scraping and flushing out dirt and soil from the building's surroundings until the dosimeter returned to a safe level. Much of the radiation particles were carried away by winds and snow far beyond the twenty-kilometre radius of the nuclear power plant and accumulated in dust and soil around buildings, nestling hotspots across the region.

Abe's initiative has inspired people in neighbouring cities to take up their own cleaning efforts. However, because no one was willing to accept the highly contaminated soil that was collected from hotspots, they were undertaken by Koyu Abe himself who had them sealed in barrels and stored on a hill behind his temple. When asked whether he was scared of piling up radiation waste in his backyard, Koyu replied:

> Living in this world, suffering is inevitable. Of course, I am scared of the radiation, everyone needs to be scared of it. It is akin to invisible snow that keeps falling and never melts away, putting all our health in jeopardy. It freezes my heart whenever I think of the long-term effect it has on our children if we don't do anything about it. Someone has to accept this soil. As a monk, my work is to help alleviate the sufferings of others. So, this is my work. And it's the very least that I can do for others.

Such disposal measures were initially meant to be temporary but a decade has passed, and neither the government nor the nuclear plant operator, Tokyo Electric Power (TEPCO), have offered a solution or lent a helping hand to manage those waste. As of March 2020, Koyu wrote (original in Japanese):

> There are about 40,000 tons of contaminated soil in the mountains behind our temple, and almost none of it has been sent to the interim storage facility. Even the so-called interim storage is located within Fukushima. So, what's the difference?

Some of the wild vegetables harvested from our mountains
are already recording an increasing amount of radioactive
substance. I feel like the current administrations have no real
intentions of facing the music, rather they are only manipulating
the situation for their own convenience, repeating cliches
like 'reconstruction and recovery' without any real actions.
Instead of directing our anger at those who are painting the
wrong image of Fukushima, we should direct our anger at
the politicians and electric power companies that are pushing
for the restart of nuclear power plants. Every time I come to
think of our beautiful hometown of Fukushima before the
nuclear incident, my heart is broken to pieces.

When crises happen, you get to see the best and worst of humanity.
The divide in Japan is sharp. Those in power and distanced away
tend to dehumanize Fukushima, acting and viewing this alien
prefecture as a necessary sacrifice, much to the similarity of
Omelas. The nuclear plants in the outskirts of Japan were built
to generate enough power supply for the heavy-duty usage of
metropolitan cities. People outside of Fukushima benefitted most
from the power plants, yet those within suffered the most. On
the other hand, there is also a glimmering hope of humanity seen
in people like Koyu and among other volunteers who came from
all around Japan to help their counterparts and who took on the
problem as their own.

Before the end of the Q&A session, I raised my hand and
asked Abe-sensei. 'Today everyone talks about globalization,
interconnectivity, and the importance of living as one. But how
exactly should we live as one?'

Abe sensei picked up a cup of tea and took a slow gentle sip.

'The answer is within a cup of tea. This is how you
should live.'

I was taken by surprise. It was one of the awkward moments
in life when you were still standing and waiting for the speaker to

continue with his explanation, and everyone's gaze was pointed at the equally puzzled translator. But nothing ensued! That was it. 'Erm . . . *arigato gozaimasu, sensei,*' I thanked him with a bow and sat down. He was giggling. I guess we're accustomed to receiving elaborated, 'intellectual' answers, but sometimes the most profound answers are found in simple gestures. They are communicated intuitively. It was a strange feeling. I was equally confused, thunderstruck, and inspired. This is the power of a single Zen allegory.

Years later, I revisited Abe sensei's gesture by chance. One day while making tea for myself in a quiet room, I saw my own reflection in a cup of tea, and I recalled Koyu Abe's explanation of the word *kizuna*. In this cup of tea, I saw *kizuna*, the spirit of 'solidarity, interconnectedness, and hope'. I saw sensei in me, and I saw myself in him. We were connected across time and space through this simple act of sipping a cup of tea. In fact, the whole universe was contained in it. Nature has nourished this ancient medicinal plant *Camellia Sinensis*, or simply *cha* 茶, and allowed it to flourish for thousands of years before they were being harvested in Yunnan. Some farmers have carefully plucked its leaves and processed them. I felt their presence within this cup of tea. I felt the aging of the tea, perhaps in a warehouse for years before being given to me as a gift. I contemplated how this cup of tea was connected to its source, packaging, delivery, the teapot that I was using, the boiled water, the right timing to steep the tea, and an infinite number of other factors that ultimately contributed to its existence and unique taste. Just as no person could ever step in the same river twice, no two cups of tea will ever taste the same. And at that moment, my heart was filled with boundless gratitude. *Everything is indeed interconnected.*

'What I fear most is the destruction that we are causing on this planet Earth. Even though the contaminated waste is now kept on the hillside behind my temple, it will still go on to affect the surrounding soil, trees, water, birds, and other animals that live there, which will continue to spread on and on. We might feel temporarily safe for now, but we must not let our guards down. We should constantly reflect on our actions and see how they will have an impact and consequence on the lives of others,' Koyu Abe had told us. The same applies to the effect of climate change and biodiversity loss in today's world. The true meaning of *kizuna*, of interconnectedness, I realized is to be embodied and flow in one's day-to-day life.

The week-long exchange programme in Fukushima came full circle with an opportunity to connect and give back to the local community. Our visit ended with a tea-serving ceremony for elderly folks who were being evacuated to a makeshift shelter. Many of them had lost their loved ones in the tsunami or had no choice but to desert their homes in the wake of the nuclear meltdown. We helped tidy up the place, served tea, and cheered them up with cultural performances. For the rest of the time, we went around the room practising deep listening. The organizers had told us, 'Lend your ears and kind attention to whatever they wish to say without judgement. Don't ask questions that might provoke unwanted memories of the past. What they need most is genuine human touch and love.'

When practised with goodwill and an open heart, attention can be life's most precious gift. It was a special feeling when both givers and receivers benefitted from the experience of being fully present. In Fukushima, I've seen how it could transcend language barriers, heal wounds of the past, and move people to tears. Through the eyes of these senior citizens, I saw strength and hope for the future. I saw *kizuna*.

Note: *Kizuna* 絆 is a Japanese kanji character:

絆 (*kizuna*): 糸 + 半
糸 (*ito/shi*): to thread, weave, or tie
半 (*han*): halves

By weaving (糸) two halves (半) together, one can, over time, braid a strong network of human bonds (絆) that is analogous to a textile fabric—resilient and capable of not only withstanding stress and tension but also serves as the fundamental basis for beauty to emerge as seen in intricate embroideries and cross-stitches.

Ask My Heart. Be Intentional

Upon returning to Malaysia, I fulfilled my promise and gave a presentation about my learnings in Fukushima to my patrons. After that, I graduated from high school and came face to face with my own personal crisis: Where is my next destination? However, my experience in Fukushima has opened up new doors of possibilities, connections, and perspectives that I had never thought of.

'What about studying in Japan? If you come here, we will do our best to support you.' I remember the encouragement of Koya Matsuoka, one of the organizers with whom I forged a close relationship during the programme.

I submitted my applications to several universities in North America and Asia, including a liberal arts programme at Matsuoka-san's alma mater, Waseda University. By a process of elimination, my crisis was eventually simplified to the dilemma of choosing between a fully funded scholarship to study environmental engineering in Taiwan, or a tuition waiver to pursue a liberal arts programme at Waseda University. Torn between Taiwan and Japan, I confided in a wise friend on this issue. He told me that I've made a huge mistake consulting him when there's only one true source where I could find all the answers.

'Let's just put the financial burden aside for a while. Ask your heart: which path would you choose, and why?'

I thought for a while and replied, 'Waseda. Because I felt connected to Japan during my first trip to Fukushima and I became interested in its culture. I want to pick up a new language, study aikido, and learn about the historical complexities of Japan—how it has transitioned from a war-ravaged country to a well-mannered, peaceful, and developed first-world nation. Furthermore, I would love to pursue a liberal arts education because I still don't know what I want to major in yet, and this would allow me to explore different fields and disciplines. Waseda seems like a perfect fit but . . .'

'Go ahead. You won't regret it. Do you want an easy life or a harder but more fulfilling one?'

'A fulfilling one.'

'Listen. If you have no appetite for a subject that you're about to study, even if you feel financially secure and comfortable for the next four years, you will not enjoy life. It will be a torment to your heart and soul. But if you love the course that you're about to pursue, I'm sure you will thrive and excel in it. And as you said, you get to learn a new language in its very native country, this will be a life-long skill that will come in handy in the future. By hook or by crook, I believe you will find the resources required to complete college. Choose the harder path, even if it means more sacrifice, even if you have to borrow some money from people, do it. Your family and friends will help because this is for the sake of education. You can always opt to pay back in the future. Secure whatever preliminary efforts that will get you to Japan. Once you settle down, things will unfold naturally.'

'But remember this: analyse your priorities, set goals, and achieve them. Money is probably your biggest hurdle at this moment. After arriving in Japan, you will need to sustain yourself financially. Gather enough money to finish off at least your first year of studies, then study hard so you can apply for scholarships. Once you master some Japanese, find a part-time job to support your living expenses. The overall process may be tiring, but four years later, you will look back in time and be proud of what you've done. This is what makes life meaningful. You won't regret it.' He dissected the path of going to Japan into actionable steps that I should focus on one at a time.

'Oh, and one more thing, the most important part of a university, I believe, is the social aspect of it. Don't forget to make friends along the way. Life abroad needs earnest support and the good company of people. Gain new experiences, cherish the opportunity, and learn as much as you can. Most people waste almost half of their time idling when we could have more efficiently utilized that time to read a good book, pick up a skill, or learn something new. Use your resources wisely. Be intentional.'

That night, I went home feeling inspired. I read a quote from *The Alchemist* by Paulo Coehlo: 'When you [truly] want something, all the universe conspires in helping you to achieve it.' I closed my eyes and smiled, 'I'm going back to Japan.'

Man walking in solitude under the moon
Artwork by Author

Chapter Five

僧伽先那

Sanghasena: The Spiritual Warrior

In 2014, about a month before leaving for Japan to pursue my undergraduate studies, I took an unexpected journey to an off the beaten path high up in the Himalayas of northern India—Ladakh, 'the land of high passes'. One of my mentors, Dr Victor Wee, was organizing a trip for donors to visit the Mahabodhi International Meditation Center (MIMC), a non-profit organization founded by a social reformer Buddhist monk named Sanghasena, and offered to bring me along as a graduation gift. My task was to assist him during the trip and help carry his camera equipment. I had no inkling of the place I was going to, no clue about the weight of his camera bag (two Fujifilm cameras packed with five different lenses and a tripod stand), nor the effect that it would have on my life later on, but I said yes immediately.

Arriving at the Leh airport was an exhilarating experience. From the plane's window, we were greeted by the panoramic view of trans-Himalayan snow-capped mountains with villages and green belts interspersed at several locations. As we landed at 10,682 feet above sea level, the sun was scorching hot, but under the shade, it felt chilly. The wind was strong and dry. My heart pounded faster than usual, and I had a slight feeling of euphoria, the kind of 'high' you get when you're tipsy. Venerable Sanghasena and his students were there to welcome us with flowers. He told us to put down our bags and luggage, and let his students carry them for us. We learned to accept the mountains as our greatest teachers—the moment we arrived in the Himalayas, they taught us to let go of our burden, to relax and learn how to breathe again, like a newborn.

'If your body is fully rested, you will be fine for the rest of the journey,' said Sanghasena. For the next two days, we were instructed to sleep as much as we can, avoid showering, drink lots of water and pee (you've got to let it out!). If bored, read, chat, or take gentle walks. Some people exhibited symptoms of headache, nausea, and shortness of breath the following day, but everyone was basically acclimated by day three. Over the next two weeks, we toured around Mahabodhi and visited its satellite schools in two remote villages. Sanghasena and his young assistant, Stanzin Gurmet, a graduate from Mahabodhi's residential school, accompanied us along the journey, guiding us through morning meditations and sharing his personal stories and insights along the way.

Ladakh can be described as the land of four Ms—Mountains, Monks, Monasteries, and Military! Once an ancient Buddhist kingdom located on the rooftop of the Himalayan plateau bordering Kashmir and Tibet, it is a remote region covering valleys of cold arid desert populated by mixed descendants of Indo-Aryans, Dards, Tibetans, and Mongolian herders and farmers. Here, one is easily swept away by the breathtaking scenery of ornate ancient temples, stupas, and peaceful monks walking against the backdrop of snow-capped mountains, but paradoxically it is also one of the most highly militarized zones in the world due to its strategic location and disputed borders between India, China, and Pakistan. Apart from tourism and the traditional economy of cultivating grains and raising yaks and pashmina goats, a great number of Ladakhi men were drafted into the military. Sanghasena himself was a rebel, a renegade who in the prime of his adolescence dropped out of school to join the military, and then deserted the army to become a Theravada Buddhist monk in Bangalore.

Born as Tsering Anchuk in a small village called Tingmosgang, Sanghasena grew up with all kinds of bizarre questions. 'Where do airplanes come from? Why is there only one sun and moon in this world? Why are some humans intelligent, others dull? Who inhabits the stars to illuminate them?' When he became a soldier, he asked. 'Who is our real enemy? What are we really fighting for?' His inquisitive mind ultimately led him down the path of spirituality and meditation during which he found so much insight and blissfulness that he wanted to spend the rest of his life as a peaceful yogi in the mountains.

'Well, living in solitude is not a bad idea, but you're a young fellow,' his teacher, the prolific writer Acharya Buddharakkhita told him. 'You owe something to the society, go and do something meaningful for your people.' He was thus given the name 'Sanghasena', a warrior of the spiritual community, and called forth to channel his military spirit of perseverance and discipline towards the betterment of others. With his rifle replaced by a saffron robe, Sanghasena embarked on a new journey to transform his meditation practice into compassion-in-action. 'What the sun is to the flower, meditation is to the mind. If meditation is lighting the candle within; compassion is sharing the light with others,' Sanghasena told us in a conversation.

Upon returning to Ladakh in the 1980s, Sanghasena saw the place that he came from drastically transformed as it opened up to the outside world. In the book *Ancient Futures: Lessons from Ladakh for a Globalizing World*, the Swedish linguist Helena Norberg-Hodge wrote about the negative effects of a new economy that was being introduced to Ladakh based on capitalism and Western modes of development—how it was breaking down the social fabric of local interdependence, eroding self-identity and well-being, and causing huge environmental damage to the natural world. Being one of the very first native Ladakhis to be self-taught in Hindi and English and exposed to the outside world, Sanghasena knew inside out the shortcomings and strength of his indigenous culture. He had experienced the hardship of living in the biting cold of the Himalayas, he knew the challenges they were facing in the midst of rapid globalization and realized the need for a new organization to foster holistic education and social reformation. Even though his initial resolution was to teach meditation to local folks, thus the name Mahabodhi International Meditation Center, it quickly spun off into a one-man humanitarian effort to alleviate suffering and provide education to students from the farthest reaches of the Himalayas.

> The best religion for the hungry and thirsty is food and water. The best religion for the sick is the doctor and medicine. For the homeless people, it is a basic home to protect them from the severe climate in the Himalayas. And for the children it is good education to actualize their potential. These are the basic priorities we must fulfil before delving into the practice of meditation and high philosophy.

At the very beginning, Sanghasena leveraged his personal connections to send a few selected boys to his teacher's school in Bangalore for formal education. He then travelled by foot to some of the remotest villages and single-handedly picked twenty girls from among the poorest families to be educated at Mahabodhi. These girls shall become the first generation of literate women in Ladakh to inspire others, Sanghasena thought. But there was no infrastructure nor teachers available at that time, so he decided to build a girls' residential school himself.

'It all began from a voice in my heart. Go ahead, you don't need millions of dollars to start your work. What you need is some piece of paper and a pen to write down what you actually want to do, print out a simple booklet, and distribute it to people.' Sanghasena told us.

He soon found a piece of 250-acre desolate and barren land provided by the Saboo Village—supposedly haunted by ghosts and wolves—and started clearing up patches of land. Tents were set up, a few bare walls were raised, and classes were conducted in succession. Holding the hands of his adopted daughters, Sanghasena taught them how to thread the delicate path of modernization while still sticking to their traditional roots and culture. These mindful steps were taken one step at a time, together as a family. On one hand, he continues to walk into hidden villages in the far-flung corners of Ladakh, sometimes staying put for days in tents with nomadic tribes to understand their needs, and along the way, selecting elderly folks and needy children to receive care and education at Mahabodhi. On the other hand, he walks around locally and internationally with his alms bowl asking for pennies to support his cause. His compassionate voice and footsteps reverberate like ripples of water that draw others to tango with him in the practice of compassion-in-action.

Sanghasena's dream has no boundaries, and he never grew tired of writing, speaking, and walking. As funds came in, so did more students and volunteers. Programmes and infrastructure projects sprouted like wildflowers across the 250-acre land. A brick-and-mortar girls' residential school and charitable hospital were first constructed in 1992, followed by a boys' residential school in 1996, then a residential school for the visually impaired, two branch schools in remote villages, a hospital, nunnery and monastery, the very first home in Ladakh for the aged and destitute, a retreat centre, and an international guesthouse for visitors from abroad. More recently, a hospice centre was constructed to provide end-of-life care. Today, Mahabodhi is a green oasis of vibrant community amid the arid desert landscape.

Sanghasena leading his students on a walk around the campus

On an early morning, we were joined by hundreds of students in group meditation, who later scattered around the vicinity. If you walk around Mahabodhi, you will spot a dozen kids running, yelling, and sweating like horses on the soccer field; several boys and girls patiently and heartily tending to Sanghasena's bed of flowers outside his lodging and many others studying meekly in their dorms. This is a diverse campus. Culturally, ecologically, and socially. Students of all faiths—Buddhists, Christians, Hindus, and Muslims study together under one roof without any incentive to convert one another. Thousands of trees including poplar, willow, apricots, and apples; flowers, vegetables, and shrubs thrive in every corner of the campus. These greeneries are watered by a highly efficient drip irrigation system, sponsored and designed by a Malaysian donor and engineer, and now administered by senior students of Mahabodhi. As we arrived at the home for the aged, we were joined by a few students who dropped by after school to volunteer and chat with their adopted *memeley* and *abiley* (grandpa and grandma). Far away from their blood relatives, many of them find solace in spending time with the elderly folks whom they see as their extended family.

Eshy Spaldon, an old grandmother who lost her fingers to frostbite, related her first encounter with Sanghasena. 'I was alone, sick, and blind. On seeing my condition near the Leh Market, Venerable brought me here and provided me with the basic necessities. He sought a doctor to operate on my eyes so now I can see properly. He has given me a new life, which I can never forget. But I don't know how to pay it back.' The rotating prayer wheel clutched between her deformed hands accelerated with greater intensity as she expressed her gratitude—perhaps she was hoping for her prayers to reciprocate the deeds of her benefactor. By keeping together the young and the old, and the able-bodied and those with disability, Sanghasena created an interdependent, nurturing, and integrated community that mirrors the dynamics of Ladakh's indigenous community—a *kizuna*.

It feels mind-boggling to chat with some of the pioneer alumni—especially a few from the very first batch of twenty girls who graduated from Mahabodhi and later returned to pay back the kindness they received. Kunzang Dechen is now a trained yoga teacher and manages Mahabodhi's Sambodhi Retreat Center and its meditation-yoga programmes. Tsewang Dolma graduated with degrees in psychology and education, and now serves as the principal of Mahabodhi Residential School. Over a meal, she could talk endlessly about the untapped potential of her students and a sense of personal responsibility for their future success. Dolma remembers the tribulation of walking mile after mile from Mulbeck Village in Kargil to arrive at Mahabodhi—the feeling of anxiety and hope for the unknown future harboured within her tiny palpitating heart, the sadness and tears that came rolling down her cheeks when she waved goodbye to her affectionate father, and the feeling of being empowered intellectually, socially, physically, ethically, and spiritually by a holistic education laid out by her guruji. These memories and experiences instilled in her the faith, empathy, and courage to continue the work of Sanghasena and to support other students at Mahabodhi. Through the eyes of these bright souls, she sees her younger self and feels compelled to channel the same love and wisdom to them that she received from her teacher. Just as the light of a candle is passed on from one to the next without extinguishing the former, compassion multiplies as it flows.

Sanghasena knew by heart the name and stories of each boy and girl who studied at Mahabodhi, and it often brought him joy and pain as he saw their wings mature and they flew off into the distance. Many of his students have become doctors, engineers, administrators, artists, and entrepreneurs. Some returned, some didn't.

'He has very high hopes and expectations for all of us to excel, but he never questioned our career path and encouraged us to live our dreams,' Stanzin Gurmet told me during our last bonfire chillout at Tingmosgang Village. Over the two weeks, Gurmet and I developed a special rapport and trust for one another. He was enrolled in the boy's residential school in 1998 and was among the first few senior boys to graduate and pursue his dream of studying film-making and mass communication in New Delhi. Feeling both inspired and indebted to his teacher for sponsoring his full education, Gurmet returned in 2012 to work for Mahabodhi as the executive secretary—his job description was impromptu and undefined. His work ranges from accompanying Sanghasena's tours around the world to making videos, hosting visitors from abroad, and managing the Mahabodhi youth wing's alumni network.

'Venerable Sanghasena's vision and energy is sometimes beyond comprehension, we often find it hard to keep up with his footsteps. It is tiring, but the work is extremely rewarding.'

'Let me know if there's anything I can do to help out and stay in touch after I settle down in Japan,' I said.

'Thank you, brother. Seniors like Dr Victor Wee have been very supportive to us morally and financially. But we still lack human resources. You being a youth, I see the spirit and potential to help in a different way. I wish you all the good strength and wisdom for further progress in your studies.'

Our bowls clinked. Gurmet had secretly sneaked a bottle of *chhaang*—a barley-based local alcoholic beverage that is consumed on almost every special occasion in Ladakh—for me to try out. It felt otherworldly to share our stories around a fire hearth on a chilly night on the top of the world and to witness in person the fruits of Sanghasena's vision turned into reality. So many lives have been touched and improved over the course of three decades with such frugal resources to begin with. The million stars above us brought to mind the expanse of the universe and the vastness of human potential, while the sound of a flowing river nearby reminded us of the passage of time and meandering path to come.

'Do you know what's the most beautiful thing on this planet?' Sanghasena asked.

'Flowers. Flowers are the most beautiful because they naturally shine and bring happiness and beauty to their surroundings. Right? But flowers cannot speak, they cannot walk. Human beings, when our heart is purified and filled with compassion, we become walking flowers and talking flowers. I wish you to become a walking flower.' This was Venerable Sanghasena's parting message to me.

Vimalacitta, a disciple of Sanghasena and the author, enjoying the
beauty of nature, Ladakh 2014.
Photo taken by Joshua Khoo.

Author with Ven. Sanghasena, Ladakh 2018.
Photo taken by Stanzin Gurmet.

Chapter Six

花之流

Striving to Be a Walking Flower

Walking Flower
walk·ing flow·er | /wɔkɪŋ flaʊər/ /wɔkɪŋ floʊər/
noun
1. Someone who shines beautifully, peacefully,
   and naturally wherever they go, just like a flower.
2. Someone who walks the Dao of Flow.

The four years of my undergraduate life went by in the blink of
an eye. Perhaps time was distorted because I was in a state of
flow, or at least I was striving my best to be a walking flower.
I entered freshman year at Waseda University feeling excited to be
back in Japan. The warm memories of Fukushima came flooding
back to me when I saw Koya Matsuoka receiving me at the
airport. Simultaneously, I was also empowered by my then recent
experience in Ladakh. Sanghasena's tale of cultivating compassion
(embodiment), of putting compassion into action (flow), and
manifesting a harmonious end result of collective compassion as
attested at Mahabodhi (regulation) served as a constant reminder
for me to grasp each unique opportunity to grow, contribute, and
actualize my potentiality as a human being. In Japan, I picked up a
quote from the historical fiction *Musashi* by Eiji Yoshikawa:

> A serious student is much more concerned with training his
> mind and disciplining his spirit than with developing martial
> skills. He has to learn about all sorts of things—geography,
> irrigation, the people's feelings, their manners and customs,
> their relationship with the lord of their territory. He wants to
> know what goes on inside the castle, not just what goes on
> outside it. He wants, essentially, to go everywhere he can and
> learn everything he can.[1]

This aspiration has motivated me to be as curious and resourceful
as possible—to pick up new languages, take a wide variety of
courses in the social sciences, arts, and humanities, talk to people,
and try to deepen my understanding of Japanese culture, both
contemporary and traditional through activities such as aikido,
zazen, and kyudo. Each summer, I would take the Shinkansen
down to the countryside of Shizuoka Prefecture and stay over at
Matsuoka's home—a family temple at the foothills of Mt Fuji.
Waking up to the sight of the mountaintop had always been a
blessing, for it is usually visible only for a short period of time and
quickly disappears behind the fog. The locals say that on an average
day, there is a one-third chance you will get to see the sacred
mountain in its entirety. I was often treated to a good meal and
some home-concocted plum wine after helping out with simple
chores, and immensely enjoyed my time there as their adopted
son. Our communication continues to evolve, from exchanging
English phrases and kanji characters on paper in the beginning,
to constructing simple Japanese sentences and finally conversing
in complete fluency on the day of my graduation. Unbeknown to
me at the beginning of this journey, I would soon be introduced
to one of the most important mentors in my life: David Holley.

---

[1] Eiji Yoshikawa, *Musashi*. Translated from the Japanese by Charles S. Terry.
(Tokyo: Kodansha International, 1981).

David Holley: The Dao of Journalism, Teaching, and Living

'An exemplary person (*junzi* 君子)
is at ease and forceless (*wuwei* 無為),
free from cleverness and deceit.
This is said to be the quality of emptiness (*xu* 虛) and simplicity (*su* 素).
To respond without subjective preconceptions,
and act without self-seeking.
These form the principles of accordance (*yin* 因).
Yin means letting go of one's self and being attuned to the true nature of myriad things.
To respond from empathy, rather than preconceived notions.
To act based on reason (*li* 理), not from desire.'

—*Guanzi*[2]

In Japan I felt most fortunate to have met David Holley, a professor turned life-long mentor who would change the course of my life and inspire me to live more Daoistically. Prior to teaching, David worked as a foreign correspondent for the *Los Angeles Times* and has indeed embodied Musashi's quote of going everywhere and learning everything he could, not to mention also going beyond that to cover from these places some of the most historic events of our era. At Waseda, he taught courses on regional history and politics based on his personal experiences and stories of living in Beijing, Tokyo, Warsaw, and Moscow. While the great samurai Musashi is known for pioneering the ambidextrous techniques of combating with two swords using both hands, David's embodiment of the Dao is analogous to a single double-edged

---

[2] 「故曰君子恬愉無為, 去智與故, 言虛素也。其應非所設也, 其動非所取也, 此言因也, 因也者, 舍己而以物為法者也。感而後應, 非所設也, 緣理而動, 非所取也。」《管子・心術上》

sword—a penetrating force of non-duality that transcends simple good and evil in seeking the truth. Sharpening and wielding such a sword is not in order to kill the enemy, but to constantly cultivate one's mind to dispel ignorance, allowing one's actions to be guided by the wisdom of impartiality instead of self-interest.

David unpacks complicated history and current affairs to students in the same way a journalist would explain hard topics to the general public from square one, with a strong sense of integrity. He is irked by reporters who actually knew better but chose to go for the hype and conflict in their writing instead of trying to explain the real situation, which is often less 'juicy' but more 'complicated'. David complained:

> Almost 100% of good big newspaper journalists in the United States care much more about their own career than the impact of their articles. What that translates to is that the bias in American journalism is to try to have your story appear to be as important as you can make it appear. It's what I call the Page-One Bias.

Today, this Page-One Bias is reincarnated in the form of clickbait headlines in the world of digital journalism. If one wants to be a well-informed, sophisticated reader, he or she has to consciously seek out competing viewpoints in the digital media and develop the ability to discern between truthful reporting and unreliable and non-factual material.

A symbolism David subscribed to and expressed in his journalistic work and teaching is the Dance of Shiva Nataraja—the Hindu sculpture representing everything good and bad in the universe dancing in an eternal loop, much like the yin and yang totem in Chinese cosmology.

> I think if we want to deal successfully with problems of the future, we have to look honestly at both the beauty and ugliness of the past. Suffering is going to happen and it's not

always clear who's the good guy and who's the bad guy. It's not really a clash between good and evil. It's kind of the universe unfolding, human history unfolding.

With this in mind, David approaches his work with a combination of concern and detachment. He knows when to be adamant in digging out and explaining the truth or reasons behind certain events, and when to let go and allow his audience and students to make their own judgment. At the heart of his teaching lies a passion to convey not just the facts but the causes for how and why things unfolded the way they did.

Throughout my four years of undergraduation, I listened to David explain in length social factors that gave rise to Trumpism in the US, the dirty role Americans played in the making of post-war Japan, the schizophrenic nature of US foreign policy shaped by the scarred memories of the Munich analogy and the Vietnam War, the reasons why the Communist party won the Civil War in China, the enormous damage done by the Cultural Revolution, and the good and bad legacies of different political leaders, be it Barack Obama, Park Chung-hee, Lee Kuan Yew, or Chiang Kai-shek. He despised Kissinger's aggression and 'decent interval' in Vietnam, but favoured his engagement with China.

In another class, Russian history, David talked about the horrible things Stalin did, but also tried to explain how they happened and why Stalin did them, which sometimes creates its own kind of moral ambiguity.

You can't understand Stalin without understanding that Winston Churchill was an imperialist who thought that the British people should hold the Indian people in subjection and occupation for centuries into the future. Almost nobody talks about Winston Churchill that way. But that's what he was. If we don't look honestly at these other issues, then you can't understand why things happened. Because you're missing the tidal waves that are making things happen. And you can't talk about the world if you miss the tidal waves.

I remember on one occasion, David showed us a news clip from Afghanistan depicting US soldiers on patrol in an extremely poor village where kids were playing in the muddy gutters and women were covered up in black hijabs. The American soldiers looked as tough as nails in their bullet-proof vests, helmets, and automatic rifles, yet all were unable to speak the local language. David stopped the video and asked, 'Just look at the image here. Can you imagine these guys defeating the local people?' Students had mixed responses. But his point was to make us contemplate situations from a local vantage point and to prevent students from over-abstractifying global affairs.

Evolutionary psychology emerged as a recurring theme in David's outlook of the world. He talked about societal evolution from small bands of hunter-gatherers into nation-states and how humans developed a strong ability for love and cooperation with the in-group and a sense of fear and hatred towards the out-group. This 'in-group versus out-group' mentality is found across all aspects of human life and, in many cases, is perceived in the writings of journalists. All we have to do is compare *The New York Times* or CNN to *The Washington Times* or Fox News, or read up how news agencies from two different countries report about an international affair or conflict, and one would discover subtle biases embedded in some of the articles.

'In my opinion, we're hardwired for that. But what we aren't hardwired for is who is "us" and who is the "other".' David strongly believes that in today's world, we ought to include all people, including those alive now and future generations, within the 'in-group', and a lead-in to that direction is to help those who see themselves as cohesive groups in tension or conflict with other groups recognize the importance of understanding why others think or act the way they do.

In fact, his entire journalistic career was an attempt to do that—to explain to Americans others' perspectives, whether it's the Chinese, Russian, Japanese, etc.; and vice versa. This vocation extends into his teaching career. David once told us:

> It would help a great deal for people of goodwill to try their best to make people on both sides understand the complexity of arguments that are unfolding, because in most conflicts, there's a human nature, a tendency to view the facts that fit your own side, your own benefits, and your own preconceived ideas. The media reports that way, the school textbooks are written that way, and everybody thinks that my side is right and the other side is so disgusting. But if people somehow could be encouraged to deal with complexity, it would reduce the level of self-righteousness and reduce the likelihood of stumbling into wars that people don't really want.

As a result of taking David's class on Chinese politics, I decided to pursue a double-degree exchange programme in China during my junior year. I knew that China had become an integral part of a changing political, economic, and cultural world—a superpower in its own right—and that any grand transformation that is going to take place in the future will most likely involve China. When I first shared the thought of going to China, David was delighted and supportive. 'If you've been to China and could speak three words of Chinese, people immediately regard you as a *lao pengyou* 老朋友 (an old friend of China!).' He spoke fondly of his experience learning Mandarin in Taiwan, his memories of hitchhiking across Tibet, and all the wonderful friendships he made in Beijing. 'I never felt like I was an alien. Getting through the (in-group-out-group) wall to the other side of the mirror . . . to be somebody who is part of a different society and functioning to some degree within it—that kind of experience is one of the motivating forces in my life,' David told me. I was mesmerized by his stories. Despite being a fourth-generation overseas Chinese who had grown up learning Mandarin and reading a few classics, I had never been to the Land of the Red Dragon. While it felt imperative to understand China's perspective on a lot of global issues, perhaps more than that, I felt a calling to reconnect with my ancestral homeland. I wanted to climb over that 'wall' and see what lies within. Not just what goes outside of it.

I left Japan in the summer of 2016 with a dozen other Japanese students and spent a year studying international relations at Peking University. All the while, David and I continued to be in touch. I gave him updates on my learnings and experiences abroad and asked for advice on presentations and writing, as well as his perspective on the latest happenings around the world. I shared with him the numerous people I encountered in China, including Professor Scott Rozelle, and how that led to an enrollment in the Stanford Center at Peking University and my later involvement with the Rural Education Action Program (REAP)—a month-long summer fieldwork in Shaanxi Province related to interactive parenting and measuring cognitive function of babies in rural China. David was always patient to nod and listen. He would spend hours over the phone just to make sure we fully understood an event or a concept. 'I'm very happy that it worked out well for you,' he tells me from time to time. Through his eyes and smiles, I felt a sense of devotion and love, maybe some pride as he witnessed each tiny growth I made in life.

When David's teaching career came to an end in 2021, he exemplified the Daoist way of retreating to nature and living a simple bucolic life after 'one's deed is done.' As stated in the *Laozi*:

> Be a valley under the sky.
> When one's potency or virtue (*de* 德) is ample,
> Return to the simplicity of unhewn wood.[3]

---

[3] 「為天下谷，常德乃足，復歸於樸。」《老子》

Today, David spends much of his time at a mountain cabin in a countryside village in Nagano, where he enjoys vegetable gardening, getting together with friends, and occasionally teaching English to children for fun. 'It's very, very satisfying to be growing healthy food in a beautiful place with mountains and forests around. It's mostly, again, like much of my life, something that unfolded naturally, and I had enough of an idea of what I wanted in life to kind of nudge things in that direction,' David told me. 'When I was six, seven, or eight years old, people would ask me what I wanted to be when I grew up. I would answer, I want to be a farmer. And to my surprise, here I am.'

Farming with David Holley in Kiso, Nagano

Returning to the Himalayas

One of the most unexpected events during my undergraduate years was a visit from Stanzin Gurmet in Japan before studying abroad in Beijing and a chance to work on projects with him in Tokyo during my senior year. Prior to that, I was already helping him out with copywriting Mahabodhi's website and designing a few posters for attracting donors and volunteers to visit Ladakh. Then, on a cold winter morning, I woke up to a message from Gurmet:

'I may see you in Japan in March 2016. Most Probably.'

'Huh, why? How?' I was puzzled.

'I need to pass some information brochures to Mahabodhi donors. And by the way, my girlfriend lives there.'

'What?! How did you two even start dating? Is she Japanese?' I was clearly not impressed by his primary reason.

'No no, she's Ladakhi. She used to study in Japan and now works there. We met in Ladakh this summer when she came back for a visit.'

I was amused. But I guess there is nothing new under the sun. Lo and behold, six months later, we were having dinner at an izakaya near Ueno Station. Gurmet introduced me to his girlfriend, Angmo, a soft-spoken charming lady who hails from a family of traditional doctors in the Changthang region of Ladakh. She received a need-based scholarship from the Japanese government to study in Tokyo since high school and, since graduation, she has been working as full-time staff at a hotel chain. The three of us spent a couple of hours breaking the ice and reminiscing about our time in Ladakh.

The speed of love is sometimes unpredictable. When I returned from Beijing in the fall of 2017, Gurmet had already married Angmo and moved to Japan to live with her on a spouse visa. This meant resigning from Mahabodhi and leaving behind the organization that he had been associated with for the past two decades. It was a painful decision, but a necessary one. After all, Gurmet was a layperson, not a monk. And like many laymen, he was merely answering love's calling when struck by Cupid's arrow.

'Knowing that Venerable Sanghasena is working day and night without me being able to extend my helping hand makes me feel terrible. But I also need to start prioritizing my own career development and personal relationships. What else can I do?' Gurmet told me. He felt trapped in a dilemma. After settling down comfortably in Japan with his wife and a part-time job at a bento shop, Gurmet still harboured a tremendous passion for entrepreneurship, film-making, and social engagement with his community back in Ladakh. He felt that he wasn't living up to his potential, but wasn't sure what to do and where to start. We decided to brainstorm ideas over chai.

'How about collaborating on a social business together? Perhaps we can host expeditions for people to visit Ladakh.' Gurmet suggested.

'That sounds like a great start. I can lead some yoga and taijiquan sessions, and we can arrange for participants to trek, volunteer at organic farms, and work with underprivileged communities.' I had just finished a month of yoga-teacher-training in Thailand and was searching for a conduit to apply my skills and knowledge.

'Yes! And we must bring them to Mahabodhi for meditation. I will introduce them to Venerable Sanghasena! I'm sure people will be inspired by his work.' Gurmet's eyes lit up at the thought of reconnecting with his teacher and the possibility of contributing back in a different way.

A year later we did just that. I designed a syllabus, built our website, and succeeded in bringing twelve participants from four countries to participate. Gurmet took care of interpretation, logistics, and the filming of our entire undertaking. Immense support was given from various sides. Leo, one of our participants brought a camera drone with him and donated it to us before leaving. My yoga teacher and dear friend, Jason Milne, flew in voluntarily to offer his teachings. Venerable Sanghasena was most delighted to see us, especially the return of his beloved disciple over a short summer. Despite his aging health and busy schedule, he attended to our guests at Mahabodhi and personally led us up on a trek to the top of the Heavenly Hill—a mountain behind the campus—for an early morning meditation.

'The higher you go up in the Himalayas, the fewer the human beings. The fewer the human beings, the less impurities and pollution. Feel the serenity and the beauty of the top of Himalayas. I am not against science. But here, don't be a scientist. Be a yogi. When a scientist sees a flower, he crushes it into pieces, destroys the colour, fragrance, and beauty in order to dissect and find out the composition of the flower. He researches and thinks. When a yogi sees a flower, he merely sees the flower, he enjoys the flower and he wants to become part of the flower. In the same way, today you will disperse around and meditate with open eyes. Let go of thinking. Look around this beautiful mountain, enjoy the clouds, the sunrise, and tune in to the beauty and purity of the Himalayas. Feel the mountains. Merge with the mountains. Become the immobile mountains. If you follow the instructions and meditate well, you will be rewarded with a cup of tea. I am not joking.' Sanghasena chuckled. A few students started pouring some chai into empty cups. Below the rising sun, our gazes were fixated on the sweet tea flowing out from thermoses. We cleared our throats. More than flowers, mountains, or anything else, we were eager to 'become One with the tea!'

Towards the end of the retreat, Angmo's father arranged for us to distribute free medicines to nomadic groups living near the Sino-Indian border and visit a boarding school for the children of nomads. There we spent half a day interacting with the school kids and then sat down with the village head and school principal to identify a few problems. Resources here are scarce—there is no internet, food is sufficient but not diverse, which leads to malnourishment, and the nomads are underpaid for their raw materials. The most striking issue, however, concerns the future well-being of these nomadic kids who are struggling between a traditional and formal education. We asked ourselves if there was a way we could help these kids who are separated from their parents for most of the year to preserve their roots and cultural identity while exposing them to the outside world, the same riddle that Sanghasena has been trying to solve his entire life. Gurmet promised to work with the village and come up with sustainable solutions. I shared how amazed I was at the camaraderie, discipline, and maturity displayed by these kids. As much as they needed support from us, they too had something to offer us. Away from their families, these kids are easily content with the simple joys of life and the older students take great care of the younger ones as an extended family.

'What if we brought a group of international students and these nomadic kids together? What could they teach and learn from one another?' I asked. The headmaster gave a thumbs up.

Photos from the Himalayan Education Action Program
by Spawo Foundation

The following year, we partnered with Flourish Foundation, a non-profit organization based in Idaho, and brought twelve American students to the nomadic school in Ladakh. For ten days, they participated in discussions, language exchanges, leadership workshops, and sports competitions with the local kids. The educational programme culminated in a fifty-kilometre trek with some of the older kids from Sato Kargyam to the plains of Parma where we were introduced to their parents. Everyone was split up to stay with different families to experience the nomadic lifestyle of camping in tents, milking yaks, combing goats, and collecting yak dung for fire. A special bond was forged at the end of the programme, seeing how students on both sides teared up at the sight of departure. To plant the seeds of mindfulness and environmental stewardship in these young students' minds and to build their capacity as empathetic compassionate leaders was the raison d'être for our programme, and it soon grew into Spawo Foundation—a non-profit dedicated to nurturing holistic education, wellness, sustainability, and culture in the Himalayas and beyond. Through Spawo, we continue to engage in social development with the local community—fundraising to buy books and furniture for the nomadic school; working with local craftswomen; and donating heaters to the retirement home at Mahabodhi.

So far, I've made close to a dozen trips across the Changla Pass—one of the world's highest motorable roads—to reach the nomadic school in Changthang. At the very top of the pass, I would always stop by briefly, panting and trudging my way in the thin air to reach a stupa and offer a white khata scarf, a gesture of honouring the mountains with my purest thought. During my very first visit to Ladakh, I asked for the blessings of the mountains and pledged to return as a 'walking flower'—perhaps a state of being, a path, and an aspiration that would take a lifetime of practice to be fulfilled—till the day it withers. As I reflect on this journey, I am astounded and amazed at the serendipity and surprises of life. From the time of my visit to Fukushima onwards, I felt like I was being put in a canoe on a river drifting downstream, not knowing when's the next turn, the next bump, or the next passenger joining me on this journey, but trusting that this boat will ultimately lead me towards the ocean of compassion. As Steve Jobs beautifully put it, 'You can't connect the dots looking forward; you can only connect them looking backwards. So, you have to trust that the dots will somehow connect in your future. You have to trust in something—your gut, destiny, life, karma, whatever.'

Three years have gone by since my last visit to Ladakh due to the disruption of the COVID-19 pandemic. But as I currently write from my dorm room at the beautiful Schwarzman College in China, I can hear the mountains' calling, Sanghasena's chanting, and the innocent angelic voice of my younger siblings at Mahabodhi and the nomadic school. 'Acholey! Acholey!' (big brother in Ladakhi) they would once tenderly address me. My heart glows with affection and gratitude, knowing that I had intuitively grasped what David Holley meant by the motivating force of his life—this feeling and capability of transcending an in-group-out-group wall to feel deeply connected and invested in the happiness and well-being of a dissimilar community. Just like our ego, the wall is merely a social construct. An illusion of separation. A wall to be torn down.

Photo taken with my *nomoley* (little sisters) and Ven.
Sonam on our trek to Parma Kargyam, Changthang

A Brief Timeline of My Journey

1995	Spring	Born in Penang, Malaysia
2013	Summer	First visit to Fukushima, Japan
2014	Summer	First visit to Ladakh, India
	Fall	Freshman year begins at Waseda University, Tokyo
2016	Fall	Junior year: one year study abroad at Peking University, Beijing
2017	Summer	One-month Rural Education Action Program in Shaanxi, China
		Became a yoga teacher
2017	Fall	Senior year at Waseda, Tokyo
2018	Fall	Graduate from Waseda University
		Return to Ladakh and co-founded Spawo Foundation
2021	Spring	Begins book project on *The Dao of Flow* during the pandemic
	Fall	Schwarzman Scholar in China
2022	Summer	Programme Coordinator at the Berggruen Institute
2023	Fall	PhD at UC Santa Barbara

Chapter Seven

中國

A Quick Flow of China's Geography–History

In 2017, when I was studying abroad at Peking University, I cold-emailed Professor Scott Rozelle of Stanford University to ask if I could intern with him on educational projects concerning rural China. Scott did not immediately agree. 'One idea is to join a semester of my class, and you can learn a bit more about how we view the world. Then we can discuss some volunteer work,' he wrote back. Scott wanted me first to understand how geography and other historical factors shaped China's current political–social economy and how these informed his attempt to leverage certain natural advantages to shape interventions and policy-making.

The next two chapters are related. Below, I hope you find Scott's first lecture on China's geographical–historical evolution most fascinating and engaging. I have paraphrased and sometimes embedded some of my own research to complement the lecture. I anticipate this section to serve as an open road towards better understanding the subsequent chapter about his Dao as a Development Economist (and a brilliant educator).

～

'The goal of this course is to try and make you guys think more like an experimental economist. Don't worry, you won't be needing any background in Econ 101 to understand everything. But in this class, you are not allowed to use the word "culture", hahaha, because economists believe there is always an economic reason behind every bit and piece of culture—that's our approach—even though I don't actually believe in it. Oh, and before I forget, on any day of our class at 6.30 p.m., you guys want to start keeping time. Because for every minute that I went over, I owe you guys a pizza, yeah for real. It's an economic incentive for me to keep time and for you to stay excited till the very end of the lecture. Now, back to the topic of our first class: What made China China?'

Scott Rozelle looked at a few American students who had just arrived in Beijing from Palo Alto a week earlier and pointed at one of them.

'Tell me, what's the biggest difference you saw between China and America?'

'Erm . . . culture?'

'Oh no, come on . . . I just said no culture!'

Everyone burst into laughter.

'Give me something more specific.'

Food. Population. Mandarin. The Chinese Communist Party. One Party System. The Middle Kingdom. Han Chinese. Confucianism. Words related to China were thrown out one after another. The list could go on forever. But what are the defining characteristics of China and what made them that way?

'Does anyone know the literal meaning of *zhongguo* 中國?'

'The Middle Kingdom?'

'Exactly. But why is it called the "middle" kingdom? Why not the "great" kingdom or the "beautiful" kingdom?'

'Hmmm . . .'

'Well, this, I believe, is the reason. To the north and west, there are hundreds and thousands of miles of the arid desert inhabited by so-called "barbarians" who were traditionally nomads. To the southwest, you have India, but it is separated by a long stretch of the Himalayan mountain range. To the east, you have the Pacific Ocean with coves of islands and pirates. And the south is made up of hilly mountainous terrain with thousands of isolated villages. You can well say that China is exactly in the middle of nowhere!

'Today we'll be talking about forty million years of economic history in three hours. What I'm going to claim is that, if you look at China's location, you look at its mountains, deserts, rainfall patterns, temperature, and other factors, and if you put all these ingredients together, they ultimately contribute to the making of China. You'll get the whole picture in a while. But for now, I'm gonna blame it all on plate tectonics. It was India that made China into China.' Scott grinned.

About two hundred million years ago, due to the movement of plate tectonics, Scott explained, 'India' broke away from the ancient supercontinent of Pangaea into an island and began forging northward at a rate of 20 centimetres per yer. It eventually rammed into Eurasia around fifty million years ago and the collision crumpled the landscape, pushing up seabed sediments sky-high to form the Himalayan mountain range, creating the world's highest peak, Everest. This impact also generated massive folds of mountains across China, concurrently giving birth to two of its cradles of civilization—the Yellow River and the Yangtze River—both originating in the high glacial meltwaters of the Qinghai-Tibetan Plateau and running through China proper. As we all know, the earliest sedentary villages were established along these river basins around the Neolithic period when the (first) Agricultural Revolution started and humans were exploring ways to domesticate plants and animals. In China, researchers have found a broad band of rice and millet farming stretching along the Yellow and Yangtze Rivers. Millet was predominantly grown in the dry north, and rice in the wet south. With these new calories, the human population gradually expanded, and perhaps by 5000 BP, wheat, barley, and sorghum[1] that arrived from the Middle East were also being slowly integrated into China's diverse agricultural system. But there was a huge geographical problem in ancient China.

'It's April now. When was the last time it rained in Beijing?'

'Last week?'

'Nah, that was a tiny bit of drizzle. I meant a downpour.'

'Erm, August?'

'Right. Rainfalls in the northern plains are mainly concentrated in the summer. The determinants are a combination of Siberia, the Himalayas, and solar activity.'

Here's some middle-school science, if you remember 'atmospheric circulation.' Remember, hot air rises and cold air drops. In the winter months, the Eurasian continent cools down faster than the sea. So it creates a vacuum right above the warmer sea that draws in cold dry air from the Siberian landmass north of China, which blows down and out into the ocean. This prevents any moisture from entering the continent. At the same time, the Himalayan mountain range in southwest Asia acts as a huge wall that blocks off any moisture from the Indian Ocean, thus northern China is cold and dry throughout winter and spring. You might want to prepare lots of lip balms. Conversely, in summer, because hot air above the continent rises faster, the vacuum above the continent now pulls moisture in from the South China Sea, generating what's called the East Asian Monsoon. Winds carrying moist air begin flowing into the Yangtze valleys around spring, bringing heavy clouds and storms to Southern China, which continue advancing northwest as the winds try to push over the belts of mountains in Central China. By July and August, the monsoon typically reaches the north and provides

---

[1] Sorghum's exact time of arrival in China is the subject of scholarly debate. Most agree that it arrived at least 2,000 years ago and perhaps much earlier.

modest summer rains over the plains. However, depending on solar activity and climate change, annual precipitation can be highly variable. In bad years, monsoons can die out in the central mountains, causing drought in Northern China and huge floods in the southern countryside.

'If rainfall in the north is only concentrated in the fall, and farmers have to start planting their crops in April spring, where are they going to get their water from?'

'The Yellow River!'

'You're right. So that's how irrigation started in ancient China! But here's another problem, just like the rain, the Yellow River is also extremely variable. It could be this deep one year, and this shallow the following year, depending on factors like solar intensity, the melting of glacier waters, and precipitation. This creates what's called the "upstream-downstream problem." Those living upstream have better access to water, while those living downstream enjoy more fertile soil and a higher yield of crops. When the Yellow River is abundant this year, everyone is happy. But when it's scarce, those in the upstream would take all the water they need, and those downstream would have two choices: they could either sit at home and starve to death in the winter, or, they could grab their weapons now and attack those villages upstream for food. Water is one major reason wars were waged in ancient China.'

A quote from the *Romance of the Three Kingdoms* describes the ever-changing state of China: 'The empire, long divided, must unite; long united must divide. Thus it has ever been.' There's indeed a huge correlation between China's unification, division, and the management of its rivers. As mentioned in the opening chapters of this book, Great Yu's success in taming the flood was a by-product of uniting different tribes and villages, in return, everyone was blessed with bountiful harvests, which, according to semi-mythical Chinese historiography, led to the peaceful establishment of the Xia Dynasty that was centered around the

Yellow River. This virtuous cycle of prosperity and unity lasted nearly five hundred years.

More than a thousand years later, when China was again divided, Emperor Qin Shi Huangdi expanded his territory into the south and finally, in the year 230 BC, conquered all the other warring states, unifying an even greater China that put almost all river canals and irrigation systems in the country under one strong regime control. Much less known is the significance of Qin's hydraulic engineering projects in advancing the unification of China. The construction of the Dujiangyan Irrigation System along the Min River by Qin's famous hydrologist Li Bing resembles much of Yu's method in channelling and dividing water using man-made levees and was instrumental in turning Sichuan into the most productive agricultural region in China. This was followed by the completion of the Zhengguo Canal in Shaanxi, which irrigated an additional 27,000 square kilometres of fertile land that further enabled the growth of Qin's massive army, all the while preventing the occurrence of natural calamity. 'Thus Qin became rich and strong, and in the end, unified the feudal states,' wrote the historian Sima Qian.

'This is the basis for the "Oriental Despotism"[2] theory in China. Because it's not an easy task to manage all the rivers, irrigation canals, and agriculture of a large sprawling country that's bigger than the size of the US, you need a strong bureaucracy and the smartest people in the government to manage such an intricate and extensive river system. But how do you find the smartest people in the country to do that?'

'Meritocracy.'

'Exactly.'

---

[2] A political-historical theory by Karl August Wittfogel (1896–1988) that explains how despotic governments in Oriental societies were created out of the need to manage hydraulic projects for irrigation and flood-control.

Influenced by legalism, the Qin empire was the first to implement a meritorious system based on rewards and punishment to lure intellectuals to its service. After Qin's collapse, the Han dynasty took over the government institutions almost unchanged, but switched to the adoption of Confucianism in the sphere of education and politics, and continued to develop a civil service examination that recruited the best of the best candidates across the country to staff its imperial bureaucracy. Meritocracy would stay on and evolve in China over the next 2,500 years from its initial emphasis on virtue and studies of Confucian classics, law, governance, and oratory to what we see today as the 'Gaokao system' (the Chinese examination system for college entrance) that includes subjects like Chinese, English, mathematics, science, and humanities. At present, the Chinese Communist Party still drafts some of the most brilliant students from top Chinese universities into the party and employs the best scientists and engineers to work on the country's irrigation systems and hydraulic projects.

'But it doesn't stop there. Geography not only created meritocracy and large-scale bureaucracies. It also created Chinese's ethnic mix.'

Ancient China for a very long time in history was confined only to the central plains that were mainly inhabited by the Han-Chinese who were constantly in conflict with the nomadic tribes of the north. Resources in the Gobi Desert were scarce, so the nomads' population remained small, however, they had really great horses and were effective guerrilla fighters, so the Han-Chinese could never completely vanquish them. During peaceful times, trade was exchanged; at bad times, wars were fought. But at some point in history, geography begot some of the world's fiercest and mightiest generals who would hail from these eastern steppes to conquer the world. Genghis Khan was the first one to rise and unite the confederations and built his great Mongol empire by conquering most of Eurasia. It took the Mongols six decades before they completed the conquest of China when Genghis Khan's grandson, Kublai Khan, finally crushed the Southern Song resistance and established the Yuan dynasty. This was a historic moment in China, in which for the first time, Han Chinese were put under the rule of a foreign monarch who also brought into China's map new territories that were populated by non-Han minorities—places like Xinjiang, Manchuria, Tibet, Inner Mongolia, Yunnan, and Guangxi. After Yuan, the Han rulers of Ming would forgo most of these minority-populated territories, but history repeated itself again when the Manchurians—another nomadic tribe from the northeastern steppes—toppled the Ming empire, and again annexed these same regions into the Qing dynasty. China today basically inherited most of its territory from the Qing Dynasty, the last imperial dynasty that fell in 1911.

'In other words, it was the minority empires that brought minorities into the Chinese imperial realm, which gave the current Chinese government legitimacy over those regions. At least that's how they think,' explained Scott.

During the dynasties of Song, Yuan, Ming, there was also a huge shift of Han population from the north towards the south. Before Yuan (Mongol rule), the majority of Han population was mainly concentrated in northern China. However, by the Ming Dynasty, the reverse became true. A push and pull factor contributed to such drastic change. The push is obviously from the Mongolian invasion. Many Han people migrated south and settled at the Pearl River Delta to flee the massacre and raping of the Mongolian troops. The pull, on the other hand, was the arrival of Champa rice from Vietnam around the time of the Song Dynasty that slowly enabled greater rice production through the 'terracing of the uplands and expansion of double cropping in the irrigated lowlands [which] solved an immediate food security problem, encouraged migration and a further population increase in the [wet] southern China rice-growing areas.'[3]

'These mass migrations led to a boom in population, agriculture, and economy in the relatively peaceful south. If you visit southern China today, you will notice one thing unique about it: diversity—the mountainous topography creates thousands of isolated villages and provinces in different valleys, hills, and mountains that evolve to form their own distinctive language, foods, ethnicity, and a rich variety of "cultures", you may call it. Even today, the majority of ethnic minority groups in China are mainly concentrated in the south and southwest.'

We can also argue that geography indirectly created 'governance with Chinese characteristics.' We've already talked about the rise of 'oriental despotism': the idea that a large and strong central government was necessary to manage irrigation and flood control in China. Today this large-scale bureaucracy is reincarnated in the form of the Chinese Communist Party (CCP), which directly mobilizes the nation's public policy related to social, economic, technological, and political development. However, with such a vast expanse of land and physical diversity, is it really possible for one central party to control everything? Nope. So, there's another key component of Chinese governance: decentralization.

For thousands of years, the central government actually delegated most of its tasks to local representatives or authorities who share a relatively high degree of freedom in their way of management. The mandate remains the same today: 'We don't really care what or how you do it, as long as you're effective in collecting taxes, following rules, maintaining infrastructure, and keeping the peace, you get to keep your job. Otherwise, you're

---

[3] Randolph Barker, 'The Origin and Spread of Early-Ripening Champa Rice: Its Impact on Song Dynasty China', *Rice* 4, no. 3–4 (December 2011): 184–186, https://doi.org/10.1007/s12284-011-9079-6.

fired.' This mentality of adopting 'pragmatism and a back-to-basics economic view rooted in local reality' pervaded the Chinese psyche of governance, and led China down the path of 'fusion economics', a term used by author Laurence Brahm to describe China's rational approach of not following 'one single model (nor political ideology) but rather integrates many different practices to create something new.' As Deng Xiaoping famously said, 'it doesn't matter if a cat is black or white, so long as it catches mice.'

'Here's the good news for experimental economists: geography makes experimentation within China really easy!' Scott exclaimed. 'Because China is huge, and each city or village especially in the south is isolated from one another, you can basically experiment with one place without affecting another.'

It all started in October 1978 when Deng Xiaoping made his historic trip to Japan and was impressed by its post-war industrial development. He marvelled at the sight of Tokyo, which at that time was a state-of-art cosmopolitan city, and returned to China with new zest and inspiration. In the following year, Deng ran an experiment that would change the course of China's history. Four cities on the southeastern coast, including Shantou and Shenzhen, were designated as Special Economic Zones to attract foreign investment and businesses. Shenzhen proved to be so successful that it was dubbed the 'Silicon Valley' of China and became a model for market reforms that were later replicated in other parts of the country.

Scott looked down at his watch and proudly announced, 'Yes! One minute to 6.30 p.m.! That was close. We're gonna watch some videos about China next week and okay . . . pizza's still on me! You'll get to learn more about Stanford's Rural Education Action Program in the future and how that relates to China's historical, social, and cultural context, as well as its problems! But for now, let's just call it a day. See you all next Wednesday!'

Chinese literati painting by Cui Wenhuan

Chapter Eight

羅斯高

Scott Rozelle: The Dao of a Development Economist

Based on a deep-seated love for China, a desire to alleviate poverty and a profound understanding of Chinese history, geography, politics, language, and its social implications, Scott co-directs Stanford's Rural Education Action Program—an organization that runs various social experiments, impact research, and evaluations to improve children's health and education in rural China. Since 1988, Scott has been running in-depth field work and interventions in more than 650 counties across 28 provinces and has collected more than a million survey questionnaires. Scott knows China better than the average Chinese citizen. Trained as a development economist, he was concerned with two big questions: How can China escape the middle-income trap? How can he help close the urban–rural gap?

Scott first analyzed the success of graduates from the middle-income trap such as Japan, South Korea, Singapore, Taiwan, and Hong Kong versus the trapped economies of Mexico, Brazil, Thailand, and South Africa and saw one crucial difference between the two: the quality of human capital. When making the leap into a high-income economy (and democratic systems), graduates already had a high school attainment rate of 72 per cent to 95 per cent, so their workforce was more ready to learn new skills, handle high-income jobs, and participate in civic engagement. On the other hand, countries that were trapped in the middle-income bracket helplessly grew and collapsed multiple times. They had an average high school attainment rate of only 36 per cent. When he looked at China, the number was 30—meaning it was below the average of middle-income countries—only one out of three working-age adults in China were high-school graduates. Something needs to be done. Even though 93 per cent of China's urban youths were already attending high school by 2021, rural youths—which made up about 70 per cent of the young population—were still disproportionately dropping out of high school.[1]

Scott was alarmed. Much investment was poured into teacher education, curriculum standardization, and infrastructure building at rural schools, but why are rural kids in China still less equipped to cope with the rigorous curriculum in high school? To find out the root cause of the problem, he and his team dove into the countryside.

One observation stood out starkly: elementary school kids in cities were usually enthusiastic, bright-eyed, and full of energy to learn and play; on the flip side, those in rural schools seemed more sluggish and unmotivated. 'What is the underlying problem here?' Scott probed deeper. Over the decades, he and his team discovered three 'invisible epidemics' that were impeding the learning progress of rural kids:

- Iron-deficiency anemia affected 25 to 30 per cent of rural children in central and western China, which contributed to fatigue, poor immunity, and short attention span.

---

[1] 'The Wire China: Scott Rozelle on China's Rural Problem', Stanford Center on China's Economy and Institutions, June 20, 2021, https://sccei.fsi.stanford. edu/reap/news/wire-china-scott-rozelle-chinas-rural-problem.

- Uncorrected myopia was rampant among rural children. About 32 per cent of sixth grade children were affected and couldn't see clearly what the teacher was writing and teaching.
- Parasitic worms were found in the intestines of 33 to 40 per cent of children in the southern part of rural China, sapping them of nutrients and further causing tiredness and dizziness.

In his book *Invisible China* (2020), Scott Rozelle estimates that about 60 per cent of elementary school children suffered from at least one of these diseases, thereby compromising their physical and cognitive development. To work out solutions for each of these issues, REAP worked with local policymakers, educators, and health experts to conduct a great many randomized controlled trials (RCT) across various isolated rural villages in China. Their findings were plain sailing. Besides the importance of promoting a balanced diet and good hygiene in the long run, there are some quick fixes that can easily be scaled to a national level to rectify the issues:

- Micronutrient supplements can tremendously lower anemia rate by 25 per cent and improve test scores.
- Correction of myopia through glasses can double the pace of learning of rural children.
- And finally, deworming medicine can be given twice a year, which costs only about two dollars per kid and is a cheap, safe, and highly effective remedy to eradicate intestinal worm infections—restoring kids' energy level.

The case is cracked. But wait.

'How are rural kids actually doing before they even enter elementary school? What about toddlers?' Scott's quest for the ultimate truth was insatiable.

Prompted and assisted by his friend Dr Reynaldo Martorell, a professor of nutrition and public health, Scott Rozelle decided to give it a try to test out the cognitive function of babies in rural China. In 2014, they trained a pilot team of over a hundred Chinese graduate students and dispatched them to rural Shaanxi province to administer the Bayley Scales of Infant and Toddler Development (Bayley Test), an international standardized test invented by psychologist Nancy Bayley to assess the scale of an infant's cognitive, language, motor, and social-emotional developments for babies aged six to forty-two months. When the gathered data was compiled, Scott was astonished beyond belief: more than 50 per cent of rural babies failed the Bayley test! This was compared to the distribution curve of a normal population where 16 per cent of the babies typically fall into this 'low development' category.

What about urban Chinese toddlers? Only 5–13 per cent failed the test. In other words, urban babies were not only normal, they were actually outperforming the average, but rural babies were falling behind miserably. In 2015 and 2016, REAP repeated the same test in other areas of rural Hubei and Yunnan. The outcomes were similar, if not even more demoralizing. In 2017, they further extended the scope of studies to include all types of communities with rural *hukou* households[2], including migrant families residing in cities whose kids were ineligible to attend public schools. Again, these babies displayed similar results—half the population was considered cognitively delayed. Was it due to genetics? Nutrition? Environment? Parenting? Was it a problem of nature or nurture?

---

[2] A core Chinese socio-economic institution, the *hukou* system was put into place by China in the 1950s. The hukou system divided all citizens broadly into two subsystems—one for urban residents and another for rural residents. Rural workers who migrated to the cities lack access to urban social benefits and their kids can't be enrolled in public schools in the cities.

In one of Scott's lectures, he explained to us the concept of 'the first 1,000 days of life'. Researchers have substantiated how our human brain goes through its most rapid period of growth and plasticity in the first three years of our life since conception. Like it or not, the roots of our brain's cognitive function and complex behaviours are oftentimes laid down in the first 1,000 days of our early life. One could even argue that our baseline IQ is more or less set by the age of three. Anthony Lake, the executive director of UNICEF, wrote that there are four main factors to help build neural connections and ensure an infant's healthy brain development: intellectual stimulation, nutrition, protection from violence, and protection from pollution.[3] Most of the babies in rural villages are not subjected to violence nor pollution. Whether they are left-behind children taken care of by their grandparents or living with their parents, rural babies are very much loved and protected by their caretakers. As already identified, diseases such as anemia and malnutrition are indeed a huge factor and improvements should be made to diversify their nutrition if we want to ensure the full developmental potential of infants. But the most pressing issue when it comes to China's rural babies isn't just nutrition: it's psycho-social stimulation.[4]

'When you asked a mom the question "Do you read to your kid?" do you know what her response was? She giggled. It's like the silliest thing she'd heard in her whole life, just the same way someone giggles when you ask whether they read to their cats

---

[3] Anthony Lake, 'The first 1,000 days of a child's life are the most important to their development - and our economic success', World Economic Forum, January 14, 2017, https://www.weforum.org/agenda/2017/01/the-first-1-000-days-of-a-childs-life-are-the-most-important-to-their-development-and-our-economic-success/.

[4] Sarah-Eve Dill, Yue Ma, Andrew Sun, and Scott Rozelle, 'The Landscape of Early Childhood Development in Rural China', *The Asia-Pacific Journal* 3, 17, no. 16 (August 10, 2019): 1–16, https://fsi-live.s3.us-west-1.amazonaws.com/s3fs-public/ecd_thought_paper_manuscript.pdf.

or turtles! Why should I talk or read to them when they still can't understand anything? That was how most Chinese rural caretakers responded,' Scott explained. Alongside Bayley tests, REAP also conducted questionnaire surveys to understand the correlations between parenting behaviours and the performance of their babies. Findings suggested that cognitive stimulation among rural babies was very limited. Only 4–10 per cent of moms or grandparents would read a book or tell stories to their kids and most households had either one or no book at all in their homes. They didn't realize, nor were they taught, the skills and importance of interactive parenting.

Rural Education Action Program (REAP)

That same year, in the summer of 2017, I had the advantage of experiencing first-hand Scott's discourse and theories translated into reality. After taking a semester of coursework with him at the Stanford Center, I joined REAP's team of field workers to be sent down to rural China to administer Bayley tests. Armed with a 7-kg Bayley test kit full of specialized toys, puzzles, storybooks, and questionnaires, we headed off in different directions across the nation. My team was first assigned to retest some of the babies in Shaanxi province who had just gone through an intervention—a six-month parenting training programme designed by psychology experts in REAP to progressively stimulate and develop an infant's language ability, cognitive function, gross and fine motor skills, and social skills. It was amazing to see how these kids were not only more sharp-witted and receptive to strangers, but breezed through each challenge effortlessly. After that, we spent the next month at two very distinctive locations, roaming from house to house in search of new babies aged six to forty-two months. One was up in the mountains of Shaanxi to test new sample groups from rural villages; and the other was in the urban outskirts of Beijing and Xi'an, testing babies from migrant workers' communities. The difference between the treatment group and the other two control groups was quite sharp. Rural babies were often quite shy, some could barely speak, many indeed failed the Bayley tests. There were, however, two outliers that have stuck with me till this day.

Author administering Bayley test for a toddler in Shaanxi

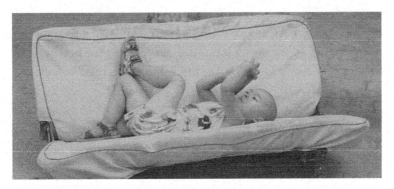

Scouting for babies age 0–3 in rural China was an interesting experience. Photo taken by author.

In one of the poorest remote villages in Shangluo, Shaanxi, and among the rural-to-urban migrant communities of Yuhuazhai in the city of Xi'an, I came across two cute baby girls who demonstrated exceptional cognitive and social-emotional performances despite growing up in very different settings. One was Xiaoyu, the other Niuniu. Xiaoyu's family farmed in the countryside while Niuniu's dad worked as a barber in the city. Their parents were busy most of the time. But during the test, both were extremely collaborative, they were excited to play and possessed a greater vocabulary size compared to others in their age group. When the test ended, their results came off at the 90th percentile. I was curious—where did their cognitive stimulation come from? I looked around and realized one common pattern, could it be that they have a loving older sister to nurture them? When we first entered their house, the older sisters welcomed us, held their baby sisters in their arms and accompanied us throughout the tests. When we left, I saw them talking and teasing one another. At that moment, I was reminded of my older brother who used to play with me when I was young and wondered how life would have been different without his company. Psycho-social stimulation comes in many forms.

Most of us grew up oblivious of the grace and favour we received in life, nor and of the impact others had on us way before our memories were formed. We tend to believe strongly in the existence of free will and self-determinism, but perhaps our intelligence and behaviours are more heavily shaped by external forces in the earliest period of our life over which we have no control. Such realization is humbling. As Malcolm Gladwell wrote in the *Outliers*, 'It makes a difference where and when we grew up. The culture we belong to and the legacies passed down by our forebears shape the patterns of our achievement in ways we cannot begin to imagine.' That tiny cumulative advantage a baby has early in their childhood, could lead to bigger opportunity, a propensity (*shi* 勢) that could contribute to greater success in life;

and it could further widen the gap between those who have it and those who don't from the very beginning.

In a recent meeting with Scott Rozelle and other Schwarzman scholars, I asked how the kids we tested were doing today. It was the year 2022, and the first batch of babies from their pilot programmes were already ten years old. Scott replied, 'after three to five years, we discovered that those who had gone through the parenting programme intervention scored 7–10 points higher on their IQ tests compared to the control group. This year, we are planning to revisit these elementary school kids to compare their math scores. The experiment is still on-going, and rest assured, our work is making an impact.' Scott smiled. I smiled.

Even though we have no control over the first three years of our own lives, we do have the power to influence that of future generations. To them, our nurture becomes their nature. Since 2014, REAP has initiated more than 50 pilot centres in various villages and townships across rural China to scale their science-based parenting programme for rural caretakers and to provide a common space where children from the age of six months to three years old can experience storytelling, gaming, and interactions with other children. For Scott, this is just the beginning of his calling to close the educational gap. He thinks that at least 300,000 centres are required across the whole of rural China and that this initiative needs to be headed not by REAP, but by the Chinese government on a national level. Cai Jianhua, a government official at China's National Health and Family Planning Commission, has taken his suggestions seriously and succeeded in ramping up free health checks and immunizations for babies. Together, they are still lobbying for the early childcare centres to become part of the government's core interest.

Everywhere he goes, Scott Rozelle continues to present REAP's research findings to academics, government officials, and business leaders. He speaks of their interest on the importance of equal access to early childhood education and high-quality human capital in order for China to escape the middle-income trap. And along the way, he continues to measure, experiment, intervene, connect the dots, synthesize new solutions, collaborate with local government officials, and present science-backed quantitative data to support his findings. Like a pine tree (*song* 松), Scott is deeply rooted in his training as a development economist and his intention to solve inequality, but he is flexible in his approach to create positive change. Analogous to Yu the Great, he identifies invisible barriers in society that are obstructing the healthy flow of a child's cognitive development, and seeks out means to circumvent them to maximize efficiency. And finally, he is constantly integrating his work within the grand scheme of things to see how projects can be implemented on a greater scale and ultimately contribute to a harmonious end goal—a peaceful and prosperous Chinese nation.

Twenty, thirty years from now, millions of children would grow up not knowing that they have averted the risk of cognitive delay with a better chance to actualize a higher potential. Perhaps they would not even know the name 'Scott Rozelle', nor the fact that they are 'REAPing' the benefits of his contribution. And really it doesn't matter. For just like water, Scott's efforts will go on to benefit and nourish countless students and generations without conscious striving. This is Scott's Dao of Flow as a development economist.

Xiaoyu and her sister in Shangluo village, Shaanxi.
Photo taken by the author.

Part III

Liu 流

Nature Flowing

行 雲 流 水

Chapter Nine

茶韻

Chayun: The Dao of Flow in a Cup of Tea

'Looking deeply into your tea, you see that you are drinking fragrant plants that are the gift of Mother Earth. You see the labor of the tea pickers; you see the luscious tea fields and plantations in Sri Lanka, China, and Vietnam. You know that you are drinking a cloud; you are drinking the rain. The tea contains the whole universe.'

—Thich Nhat Hanh

Breaking News. Aged Pu'er tea reached a record high price in Hong Kong Autumn auction . . . a 1920s Pu'er tea cake was auctioned in Tokyo and sold at 3.76 million HKD (half a million US dollars) . . . Amidst the pandemic, another brick of Pu'er tea from the 1900s was auctioned online by Sotheby's for 1.2 million HKD.

The soaring price of antique Pu'er tea is often treated as a craze and met with scepticism and disbelief. What makes Pu'er tea so special? And why would anyone want to buy an approximately 300 g antique tea biscuit for hundreds of thousands of dollars?

It all traces back to a series of events in the mid-1990s—an important turning point in the history of Pu'er tea.

In 1993, Malaysian-Taiwanese tea lover Deng Shihai first proposed a controversial groundbreaking theory about Pu'er tea in the first Pu'er Festival at Simao, Yunnan, after the post–Mao Zedong opening of China. 'The longer it ages, the better it tastes' (*yuechen yuexiang* 越陳越香), Deng said. Born in a small Malaysian town of Ipoh, Deng grew up drinking aged Liubao and Pu'er tea with his family. Pu'er tea, a variety of post-fermented dark tea native to Yunnan, China, was imported by overseas Chinese to Malaysia because of its durability, reasonable price, and aging quality. Just as it survived the harsh terrain of the ancient tea horse road to Tibet for centuries, so did it endure the long shipping journey to Southeast Asia and provide much joy and comfort to the Chinese miners and traders who missed their homeland. Over time, people also discovered that aged Pu'er tea actually tastes better than the fresh version. Leftover tea in warehouses was found to possess a kind of stale fragrance that people later came to be fond of. It was a serendipitous concept that grew organically out of empirical evidence.

Deng's theory caused an immediate uproar and a heated debate among tea experts and academics at the conference. How could a tea's flavour, and particularly Pu'er tea be enriched the longer it is stored? Some tea connoisseurs acknowledged it, but academics dismissed it as pseudoscience. The idea lost its momentum. In 1995, however, after conducting several field studies around Yunnan and visiting tea collectors in and outside of China, Deng published a book titled *Pu'er Cha*, documenting pictures, characteristics, and origin of a list of vintage Pu'er teas he had tasted produced from the early 1900s all the way up to the 1990s. This time, his publication coincided with the release of large quantities of Pu'er tea from warehouses in Hong Kong into the tea market amidst the uncertainty and fear of the British colony's handover to China. Traders in Hong Kong were eager to sell off their tea assets, and dealers from all around the world, especially Taiwan, flocked in to purchase them in bulk. Deng's publication quickly became 'The Pu'er Tea Bible'—a classic textbook used by tea lovers and traders to study, reference, and compare the packaging and taste of different antique Pu'er tea. As China became richer, enthusiasts from the mainland started going abroad to repurchase them, and the price of antique Pu'er tea continued to skyrocket. Even those who couldn't afford the antiques went into a frenzy collecting fresh Pu'er tea cakes in bulk, hoping that they would inflate decades later.

Soon, all kinds of problems started surfacing. Counterfeits appeared in the market and different schools and actors debated, contested, and negotiated about the authenticity of Pu'er tea. Another huge problem indicated that after close to three decades, many collectors were puzzled that the fresh Pu'er tea they bought two or three decades ago did not seem to taste better after storage, and found it hard to sell them back to the market. Beyond one's grasp, the price of antique Pu'er cakes, especially those from the first half of the 1900s did not plummet. They continued to rise higher than ever before. The masses became confused. They had no access to the true full story or backstory of magnates and elites. How does one define high-quality Pu'er? Is Deng's theory of *yuechen yuexiang* merely a hoax?

Author's personal tea set. Enjoying a cup of '90s Pu'er tea.

The Dao of Flow is within a cup of tea. It seems like Deng's proposition of *yuechen yuexiang* is not an absolute truth, but a partial truth. Meaning that Pu'er tea has the potential to transform and age for the better, if and only if it meets certain criteria and conditions.

Sun Bin's *Art of War* says, 'Favorable time and weather conditions, geographical advantages, and the harmony of people's effort all must be in place for victory to ensue.' Similar to the aging of wine, which is influenced by grape origin and variety, viticultural practices, winemaking techniques, bottling, and vintage, a good Pu'er Cha needs to be sourced from large-leaf tea trees from an ecologically healthy environment in Yunnan. It needs to be picked and processed in the right methodology and stored naturally in a conducive environment that is usually enclosed, dark, and humid (approx 70 per cent) for microbial enzymatic reactions to take place. If you can meet all these conditions, victory shall ensue. So the question is, what has gone haywire along this chain of supply? To understand the complexity of this issue, we must first return to Yunnan and understand its history.

Yunnan's Natural Tea Forests and the Bulang Indigenes

'Our Pu'er tea grows inside the primeval forest. It coexists with tens of thousands *mu*[1] of natural forests and absorbs the essence of heaven and earth. Therefore, the taste of Pu'er is the taste of Nature.'

—Su Guowen, the Last Prince
of the Bulang Minority

---

[1] *Mu* 畝 is a Chinese unit of area measurement. 1 *mu* = 1/15 of a hectare, or 0.1647 acres.

Su Guowen, the Last Prince of the Bulang Minority.
Photo courtesy of Josh Guo and Hannah Deng.

In the ancient woodland of Southwest China stand tall trees that have been thriving and flourishing for hundreds, even thousands of years. This is one of the most biodiverse regions of planet Earth, a culturally rich and diverse enclave that sits between Southeast Asia's tropical rainforest, the Himalayas, and East Asia. It is dubbed as the kingdom of animals and plants and the motherland of *Camellia Sinensis*, the plant that provides us with tea. Today, the oldest living tea tree in Lincang, Yunnan, is estimated to be over 3,200 years old. In the vicinity, one finds more than 1,400 lush tea plants said to be descended from this mother tree. Research suggests that tea plants in other parts of China and the world—most of which are of the small-leaf variety *Camellia Sinensis* var. *Sinensis*—actually evolved from the large-leaf variety *Camellia Sinensis* var. *Assamica* that is prevalent in Yunnan. The reason for this divergence, which occurred around 22,000 years ago is unknown. But Daoist mystics suggest that as tea plants spread further away from Yunnan—an ecological treasure trove blessed with tropical sunshine, nourishing rainfall, elevated mountains, and rugged terrain rich in organic soil matter—the 'essence' they received from Mother Nature diminished, and thus over time they evolved into smaller varieties to better adapt to a less resource-abundant environment. According to scientists, this divergence happened around 22,000 years ago during the last glacial maximum.[2]

For millennia, local indigenous people in Yunnan and Indo-Burma have lived in harmony with their tropical rainforests and ancient tea trees. Ethnic minority groups such as the Bulang, Dai, Deang, and Hani were among the first tribes to domesticate, cultivate, harvest, process, and worship tea for at least 2,000 years. The Bulang people in Jingmai are especially known to be staunch protectors of tea trees, for their fate is closely intertwined with that of tea. According to the scriptures, their ancestors once migrated from a land far away after being attacked by other tribes. During the journey, diseases started spreading, and their leader Pa-ai-neng, sick and exhausted, came to rest under a tree adorned with waxy leaves. Intuitively he chewed on some of the leaves, which tasted bitter but ended with a sweet aftertaste and he drifted off to sleep. When he woke up, he was healed and quickly distributed the medicinal leaves to everyone. Soon his people were all cured of their diseases and as a token of gratitude, Pa-ai-neng named the tree 'La' and led his people to worship the tree with utmost reverence. Regaining hope, they decided to settle down here in the mountains of La. Each time a Bulang came across a tea plant they would tie it up with wild rattan and mark its sacredness; before building a house, they would first cultivate a tea plant in the compound. An ancient proverb attributed to Pa-ai-neng says:

---

[2] Muditha K. Meegahakumbura et al., 'Domestication Origin and Breeding History of the Tea Plant (*Camellia sinensis*) in China and India Based on Nuclear Microsatellites and cpDNA Sequence Data', *Frontiers in Plant Science* 8 (January 2018): 2270, https://doi.org/10.3389/fpls.2017.02270.

If I leave you with cattle and horses,
I fear that a natural disaster will kill them all.
If I leave you with gold, silver, and treasure,
you might spend it all.
But if I leave you with tea trees, they will grow inexhaustibly
and provide for countless generations. You should care for the
trees and forests just as you care for your own eyes.
Pass it on from generation to generation. Do not let it be lost![3]

A Bulang indigene worshipping tea trees.
Photo courtesy of Josh Guo and Hannah Deng.

The Bulang indigenes' animistic belief and spiritual connection
with nature has led them to protect not only the tea trees but
also the forests and biodiversity around them. Through the
accumulated wisdom of their elders, they have developed a
comprehensive agricultural system based on the preservation
of natural tea forests, intercropping practices, and rotational

---

[3] 「我要給你們留下牛馬，　怕遭自然災害死光；要給你們留下金銀財
寶，　你們也會吃完用光。就給你們留下茶樹吧，　讓子孫後代取之不
盡、用之不竭。你們要像愛護眼睛一樣愛護茶樹，　繼承發展，　一代傳
給一代，絕不能讓其遺失。」

agroforestry. Crops are planted on a piece of farmland for one to three years, then abandoned for seven to ten years while they switch over to a new piece of land, allowing the land to lie fallow and nature to replenish the soil before returning to cultivate it. Albizzia, cassias, alder, and camphor are planted alongside tea to improve biodiversity as they help to decrease soil erosion and increase the diversity of organic soil matter. Over the course of many generations, these lands would transform into natural tea forests. To maintain the health and vitality of their sacred La plants, natural tea forests are protected and only harvested with moderation. Within a tea forest, hunting is strictly prohibited and felling is deemed a serious crime. Note that a tea forest isn't a tea plantation, but a natural forest where a large number of tea trees grow. Based on a sampling survey in 2013, at least 244 plant species were found in tea forests near Mangjing Village, which is comparable to that of natural forests nearby.[4]

Bulang Village nestled within tea forests.
Photo courtesy of Josh Guo and Hannah Deng.

---

[4] TEEBcase (2013), 'Harnessing Ecosystem Services for Local Livelihoods: The Case of Tea Forests in Yunnan, China', by L. Liang, Y. Xiang, and K. Takeuchi, https://www.teebweb.org/media/2013/10/Harnessing-ESS....-in-Yunnan-China.pdf (accessed April 5, 2023).

Famed for producing tea, Bulang indigenes and other ethnic minorities in Yunnan have been supplying tea to Tibet, Sichuan, Beijing, and other regions of China for thousands of years through the ancient tea horse roads. It was only in the early eighteenth century that Han-Chinese merchants started entering the tea-growing areas of Yunnan to set up family commercial brands that source high-quality leaves, organize fine processing for pressing the tea into cakes, and trade the products internationally. As a result, the tea cultivation area in Yunnan expanded but the ecology remained largely intact because most family commercial brands still worked closely with indigenous populations to source their tea and were strict on acquiring high-quality large-leaf Pu'er tea from natural forests to build and preserve their reputation. In fact, it was remnants of tea produced by these brands (such as *Tongqinghao* 同慶號 and *Songpinhao* 宋聘號) from the early 1900s that cost millions of dollars today. They are known to possess the quintessential essence of Pu'er's *chayun* 茶韻—the taste of nourishment from Heaven and Earth—a harmonious blend of fragrance, texture, and long-lasting aftertaste that is distinctively unique to the terroir of Pu'er tea so much so that this sensation flows deep into one's consciousness and remains there due to the effect of experiencing something uniquely harmonious.

Deng Shihai has compared Pu'er tea's varying fragrance and aftertaste to that of camphor, ginseng, jujube, orchid, lotus, etc. However, when fresh and young, a good piece of Pu'er tea may taste extremely bitter and astringent with a returning sweetness in the throat. After decades of aging, the bitterness and astringency are tamed and transformed into a harmonious mellow flavour, a smooth texture, and lingering sweetness. Therefore, the longer they are stored, the better they taste.

The Rise of Terrace Tea Plantations and its Implications

Since the Second World War, Yunnan's tea production system has gone through states of upheaval and the livelihoods of indigenous communities and family commercial brands were constantly thrown into disarray. In 1938, the very first National Tea Factory of Menghai was opened by the Republic of China's national government to improve black tea production for export purposes, marking the start of mechanical and mass production of tea in Yunnan. Advanced machines were brought in from British India to speed up processing. By the time of the founding of the People's Republic of China (PRC) in 1949, China was one of the world's poorest nations, and the new government was keen to increase economic output to build its economy. The tea industry was taken over by a planned economy that ran solely on state-owned factories, and mass production continued to expand. Many state-owned factories continued to work with the local people in acquiring raw tea materials. Some were processed in the factories, others handcrafted. Tea forests were sometimes over-picked, but *chayun* somehow remained. Some of the earliest tea cakes produced by these state-owned factories continued to age for the better, and today they are as expensive as the family commercial brands from the twenties and thirties.

The real kick in the Achilles' heel of Yunnan came in the late 1970s and 1980s when China was rapidly opening up and reforming. It brought about a new system of cultivation to Yunnan that was seen as more modern, efficient, scientific, and advanced. Many forests were cut down and replaced with either monoculture rubber plantations or narrow, uniform, and dense tea bushes arranged in terraces. Terrace tea is called *taidicha* 台地茶. They are trimmed regularly to encourage rapid regrowth for harvesting while preventing trees from growing too tall for convenient picking. The use of pesticides and chemical fertilizers were also introduced and, unsurprisingly, production output increased manifold. This encouraged even more farmers to switch to terrace tea fields and more forests being levelled, burned, and converted into terrace plantations. After the popularization of Pu'er tea by Deng Shihai and other tea actors in the 1990s that led to the Pu'er Tea boom, more local farmers were incentivized to change their traditional means of farming to terrace plantation to increase production. Today it is estimated that 90 per cent of Pu'er tea in the market comes from terrace tea plantations.[5]

Then all of a sudden, tea connoisseurs were baffled: the *chayun* of Pu'er tea was lost. Even though the whole world was in a frenzy to produce, promote, and purchase Pu'er tea, most people didn't really understand the intrinsic value of Pu'er tea nor the rationale and origin behind its value; all they knew was that 'the longer you store, the better it tastes, and the more expensive it becomes!' And while they were busy doing all that, Mother Nature was exchanging quality for quantity, and subtly and gradually losing its *qi*—vitality and essence. When many tea dealers and collectors finally came to the realization that tea from natural forests seems to have a greater tendency to age and transform and thus is more likely to embody *chayun* as compared to terrace tea, the price of forest Pu'er tea soared to about four or five times that of terrace tea in 2007, and the gap continues to widen today. That very same year, the Pu'er tea market crashed—there was too much low-grade tea in the market and too much hype and inflation accumulated from the previous few years, while demand fell all of a sudden.

Capitalism and the Dao of Flow

As always, capitalism has its invisible hand of incentivizing adaptation and change based on greed and maximizing profit. Some local farmers began mixing terrace tea with forest tea leaves and selling them at a higher price; some applied chemical fertilizers to natural tea forests to increase their production;

---

[5] TEEBcase (2013), 'Harnessing Ecosystem Services for Local Livelihoods: The Case of Tea Forests in Yunnan, China', by L. Liang, Y. Xiang, and K.Takeuchi, https://www.teebweb.org/media/2013/10/Harnessing-ESS....-in-Yunnan-China.pdf (accessed April 5, 2023).

others over-picked natural tea forests to maximize their profit. The result was continuous ecological degradation. Worse still, many local farmers decided to switch over to rubber plantations in Yunnan, which offers a more stable and profitable income at the expense of biodiversity. As the Gao family in Yiwu relates to the author Jinghong Zhang in her book *Puer Tea: Ancient Caravans and Urban Chic*:

> Tea can coexist with other plants peacefully. But rubber is like a pump. It's hard to find any other plants in the rubber forest. The earth used for rubber may become dry and eventually useless . . . The history of rubber in Xishuangbanna is less than one hundred years old. We still don't know what its impact will be, just as we still lack knowledge on aged Pu'er tea.

Now, even *chayun*, the soul of tea, is lost within natural tea forests due to overexploitation and ecological degeneration in many parts of Yunnan. The flow of essence from Heaven and Earth is obstructed. The Pu'er tea grandmaster Deng Shihai himself has spoken on this issue on many occasions and repeatedly warned against ecological destruction and the disappearance of *chayun* in Yunnan. Mother Nature is like a mirror that acts in accordance with the Dao of Flow. In order to receive, we must first learn to give—to allow tea forests themselves to receive, grow, connect, and create before they can provide us with the blessings of nature, and this needs to be carried out according to the harmonious pace and rhythm of nature as exemplified by the Bulang indigenes' relationship with their tea forests. The more society progresses, the more we fall into the trap of placing too much trust on human intelligence, science, and technology. We think that we can outsmart Nature by tweaking it to suit our needs and wants, but we often end up missing the forest for the trees (literally, and metaphorically) and end up hurting ourselves in the long run. Climate change and the disappearance of *chayun* is Mother Nature's cry to mankind that we've strayed away from the harmony of Dao. If we continue to use brute force to make Nature grow, if we use brute force to control, expropriate, extract, and exploit her, then humans are doomed to backfire. On the contrary, ancient wisdom suggests that we should use *song* 松—non-violent and non-forcing 'skilful means'—to actualize our human potential without destroying our personal and ecological harmony.

Bulang people harvesting tea

Bulang people enjoying a cup of tea while processing tea and working on other chores.
Photos courtesy of Josh Guo and Hannah Deng.

'Our people have this theory of being "lazy tea" farmers—we don't need to feed our plants with fertilizers nor apply any pesticides. All we need to do is to wait passively for the leaves to naturally grow luxuriant, and then harvest a portion of them. Paradoxically, this method's return on investment today turned out to be much higher than those who worked painstakingly [on terrace plantations]!' said San Wen, a Bulang representative on tea heritage. The term lazy here corresponds to the idea of *song*—relaxed skilful means based on wisdom. The Bulang people are by no means lazy and sluggish. When the tea trees are ready, they have to climb up at least ten metres high to pick the leaves, and conscientiously roast, roll, sun dry, and compress them into cakes. Besides tea, they also do other forms of agriculture and raise livestock to sustain themselves. Above all, it takes collective effort, grit, and faith to protect their forests from being destroyed.

Since 2006, a Bulang village elder Nan Kang has led efforts to form a local tea cooperative that includes every family household in the village. This is to prevent selfish individual gains and to keep everyone's conduct monitored, unified, and managed by the village committee. The cooperative has even come up with its own trademark Pu'er tea brand 阿百腊 *Abaila*—meaning 'the spirit of tea'. Lands that were previously turned into terrace plantations were reconstructed to mimic the environment of natural tea forests, such as by digging out and reducing the number of plants from 3,000 to 180 trees per *mu* (approx. 0.165 acres). Fertilizers and pesticides are stringently banned. If you walk into one of the village's tea gardens today, you will encounter a wide assortment of plant species, insects, and birds. A couple generations from now, these gardens would unfold into a natural tea forest. For the Bulang people, their effort seemed 'lazy' or effortless for they knew when to exert skilful force and when to relax and enjoy the breeze—*song* 松—just like performing taijiquan.

The goal here is not to romanticize indigenous culture. The slash-and-burn practices, for example, which are found in many indigenous cultures are no longer a sustainable practice in certain landscapes[6]; and many indigenous communities have also benefitted from the introduction of modern medicine, infrastructure, and education. Nevertheless, there is something we can certainly learn from the indigenous world view of seeing spirituality in everything, of treating nature as sacred, and of keeping in mind the interconnectedness of all aspects of life—something that is lost in our current society. By illuminating the intimate connection between the artistic value of tea and nature, I hope that we can perceive the Dao of Flow within the story of Pu'er tea and the Bulang indigenes' spiritual milieu, and distill for ourselves a new perspective, a new-found wisdom or framework that is worth embodying, flowing, and harmonizing in our life. One framework is the idea of 'circularity' or 'circular economy'—a nature-based model of production and consumption that is restorative and regenerative by value and design. While most indigenes have inherited such a mode of thinking and practice for millennia, there have also been inspiring case studies in recent times to reintroduce circularity into our modern way of living.

---

[6] Slash-and-burn practices in Indonesia have caused death and massive air pollution (haze) in Southeast Asia. However, it is worth noting that Native Americans have skillfully used indigenous burning and 'good fire' for ecological purposes and land management for thousands of years. For more information, see: Kimmerer, R. W., and F. K. Lake. 2001. 'Maintaining the Mosaic: the role of indigenous burning in land management.' Journal of Forestry, v. 99, no. 11, pp. 36–41.

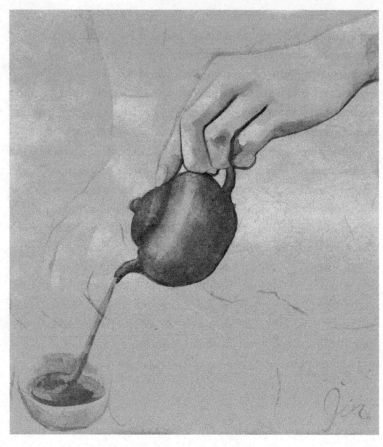

Flowing Water. Nourishing Tea.
Gift from Thai-American artist Ariana Chaivaranon

Chapter Ten

循環・本土

Circularity and Localization:
The Shimosato Model

'The Dao of Heaven is void and formless.
Because of its emptiness, it will not be exhausted.
Because of its formlessness, it has no resistance.
Because of its lack of resistance,
it can flow through myriad things without changing itself.
Virtue is the manifestation of the Dao.
Through it, all things are born and animated.
And the mind can perceive the essence of the Dao.
Therefore, virtue means attainment,
and by attainment,
I mean that all things attain their original nature.
Thus, *wuwei* is called the Way,
and to provide is called virtue.'

—*Guanzi* [1]

---

[1] 「天之道，　虛其無形。虛則不屈，　無形則無所位<低>；無所位<低>，　故遍流萬物而不變。德者道之舍，　物得以生生，　知得以職道之精。故德者得也，　得也者，　其謂所得以然也，以無為之謂道，舍之之謂德。」《管子・心術上》

139

In 2019, my Ladakhi co-founder, Stanzin Gurmet, his wife, Angmo, and I took a ninety-minute train from Tokyo to Saitama to visit our friend Osamu-san, a full-time computer programmer who moonlights as a farmer there and is taking courses on organic farming. 'In my day-to-day work, I had to focus on tiny characters in front of the computer screen all the time. When I was introduced to farming for the first time, I felt close to nature and both my body and mind felt *sawayaka*, refreshed. From then onwards, farming has become a complementary hobby to my tedious work, a space for me to rest and slow things down a bit. Now I hope to bring this initiative one step forward and become fully organic,' Osamu-san explained to us. His words invited us to explore Shimosato Farm 霜里農場 (also known as Frostpia) in Ogawamachi. Here almost everyone is an organic farmer. As our train moved further away from Tokyo, the scenery of skyscrapers was gradually replaced by *minka* or wooden Japanese houses, and blooming flowers amongst the green forests. It was the time of spring in Japan.

Upon arrival, we were welcomed by Arii-san, a farmer at Shimosato. She was dressed in a simple brown jacket and grey cap with squared glasses. A few kids from a local family were excited to see new faces in the village and shadowed us around. Arii-san was excited to learn that Gurmet and Angmo were from Ladakh. She exclaimed, 'No way. Have you guys read the book *Ancient Futures*? We were very much inspired by this book and the indigenous wisdom of your people.' It turns out that the author, Helena Norberg-Hodge was a good friend of Shimosato's founder, Yoshinori Kaneko, and the community there was directly involved with the translation of *Ancient Futures* into Japanese (懐かしい未来). Gurmet and I smiled at each other. We were surprised at how small the world is and the way dots are beautifully connected, for we were just in the midst of designing a syllabus for our Himalayan Education Action Program to host a group of American students from Idaho in Ladakh for two weeks, and were planning to incorporate lessons from *Ancient Futures* as part of our core curriculum for students to compare and contrast the content of the book with what they see in Ladakh. We felt like the stars were aligned.

While giving us a tour around the village, Arii-san explained the workings and history behind Shimosato. Organic agriculture began here in 1970 when her teacher Yoshinori Kaneko took over his father's farm upon graduating from the National Farmer's Academy. Distressed by the news of rising global pollution, he was interested in experimenting with new methods of cultivating rice and vegetables without the use of chemical fertilizers and pesticides. He had an idealistic thought: 'If only each farmer could supply organic food to just four family households, Japan would become a self-sustainable country.' To get the ball rolling, he allocated two hectares of farmland to be converted into organic fields, and searched around for household families to sign a supply–delivery partnership contract with him, but without success. It took him close to a decade of experimentation with organic cultivation, coupled with his dedication in propagating environmental awareness through organizing book clubs and agriculture festivals, but he finally managed to set up an *Orei-sei* (お礼制) partnership system with ten household families. Just ten.

Orei-sei means a 'gift, ritual, or gratitude system' in which the price or payback of the produce is determined by the consumers according to their own will and capability—through financial remuneration or partial service at the farm. Kaneko-san was able to transcend the capitalistic model of profit maximization by replacing it with a gift economy based on trust—the maximization of value instead of profit. Each family was given 20 kgs of rice, 20–80 eggs, 15–20 kinds of vegetables and some milk per month, delivered twice a week. Presently, the *Orei-sei* system has expanded to include thirty to forty household families in Saitama and Tokyo. Much like his vegetables and rice fields, Kaneko's network and influence grew organically, so much so that it attracted the visit and award recognition by the Japanese Emperor Akihito and Empress Michiko. Since the '80s, he has accepted more than four hundred interns from Japan and abroad, and open-heartedly shared his methodology of organic farming, which he is still refining annually through trial and error, with neighbours, friends, and other farming communities worldwide. One hectare after another, and slowly all household families in his village gradually converted into organic farmers. Today, Shimasato has become a model of sustainable village transformation for the world.

The core philosophy of Shimosato Farm is built on nature's circularity and soil regeneration. Arii-san unlatched a shaft panel and explained, 'This is where all our human poops go. Here they undergo biogas fermentation and are converted into liquid fertilizer and methane for burning.' Other forms of organic waste such as chicken and cow dung manure, rice straw, fallen leaves and branches are mixed in a compost to activate microorganisms, and then used to fertilize and improve the soil, the very foundation for growing crops. A good compost must be well-aerated and is said to contain millions and perhaps trillions of good microorganisms to nourish the roots and soil for healthy vegetables to emerge. Produce from the Shimosato farm then goes back to feed the people and livestock. A wholesome cycle becomes complete and repeats itself!

One thing that distinguishes Kaneko's family from other farmers is that they are constantly developing and incorporating new green technology and experimenting with new techniques to improve their organic farms. For instance, Shimosato Farm is fully powered by clean energy. Solar panels are installed on rooftops to generate electricity for powering electrical fencing around the livestocks, drawing water from the well, providing to local households, and sometimes even selling back to the grid. Mechanical tillers and tractors for plowing the field all run on biodiesel instead of gasoline. According to Kaneko-san, nature has its own natural cycle of depletion and rejuvenation. This cycle might take a hundred years.

But the art of organic farming is to lend nature a helping hand by shortening its natural cycle and borrowing nature's force to serve our needs without disrupting the harmony of it.

'What about bugs and weeds? How do you get rid of them without using pesticides?' we asked. The answer is simple: circular balance of nature. In a healthy ecological system, harmful insects such as aphids or beetles are taken care of by their corresponding predators such as snakes, lizards, and ladybugs, whom Kaneko calls the 'knights in shining armour'. Shimosato Farm has also refined several ways to control weeds, such as using a kind of biodegradable paper mulch to cover the fields when crops are still seedlings. Remaining weeds are then mowed and fed to farm animals.

In contrast to organic farming, modern scientific agriculture pits farmers in a rat race against evolution. When chemical inputs such as pesticides and nitrogen fertilizers were first introduced in industrial farming, they were revered for increasing agricultural productivity. However, with more insecticides being used each passing year, insects become more immune and resistant towards the initial dose of pesticides, and thus, a higher concentration or frequency of usage is required to achieve the same results. Agrochemical companies began pouring more money into research and development to come up with stronger pesticides to kill unassailable insects and superbugs, and farmers became reliant on these chemicals to sustain a desirable output regardless of the increasing cost—oblivious of its invisible harm to themselves and other human beings, animals, soil, water, and vegetation. Based on research in 2020, around 385 million cases of unintentional, acute pesticide poisoning (UAPP) were estimated each year, averaging 11,000 fatalities and affecting 44 per cent of total farmers worldwide.[2]

---

[2] Clevo Wilson and Clem Tisdell, 'Why Farmers Continue to Use Pesticides despite Environmental, Health and Sustainability Costs', *Ecological Economics* 39, no. 3 (December 1, 2001): 449–62, doi:10.1016/S0921-8009(01)00238-5.

There's another conundrum. Just as soon as some farmers decided to stop using pesticides, the population of pests in their local environment suddenly shot up to levels higher than their initial baseline. This situation would remain indefinitely unless their natural predators, which were almost completely obliterated by the same pesticides that farmers used, were restored. But that could take years on end, since the ecological cycle has been disrupted. What's more, the overuse of chemical fertilizers also killed off beneficial bacteria and fungi, depleted nutrients, caused acidification and destroyed organic matter within the soil, making it even harder for farmers to 'turn over an organic new leaf'. Giving up on pesticides and fertilizers could potentially mean having zero-income for the next few years without a guarantee of success. Modern industrial farming basically kills everything and replaces them with artificial inputs that we think we can control— but in reality enslave farmers—all the while shattering ecological systems both above ground and below. This is the paradox of 'maximizing efficiency' without taking into account the bigger picture of harmony. Even though the productivity of agricultural yield seemed to increase in the short run, the true efficiency of the system as a whole has declined over time.

The maximization of efficiency through harmonious circularity and sustenance has been embedded in traditional Japanese society and agriculture for thousands of years. People use the phrase *ikasu* (活かす・生かす) to explain 'harnessing or making the best use out of something', whether it's farming a piece of land, utilizing one's tool, resources, or specific skills, and experiences for good. But there's actually more depth to the characters *ikasu* (活・生), which essentially means 'to keep alive, to resuscitate, or give life' to something. In Shimosato, we see that the harnessing of farming's true potential lies in:

土を活かす: keeping the soil alive
微生物を生かす: keeping the microorganisms alive
天敵昆虫を活かす: keeping the bugs alive

自然の力を生かす: keeping nature's force alive
人との絆を活かしている: keeping the power of human
bond (*kizuna*) alive

Like a star, with its gravitational force pulling smaller planet'
into its orbit, Shimosato Farm became the breeding ground
not just for organic farmers and biodiversity, but also for
community revitalization. Besides supplying to contracted
household families, produce from Shimosato are primarily
sold to local markets, cooperatives, or to local breweries and
workshops that process them into end-products such as sake
and tofu. Everything here is home-grown, locally processed,
and regionally sold and consumed. Urbanites have to come all
the way to Shimosato in order to see, taste, and experience for
themselves the fruits of organic farming. This model supports
a vibrant local economy that facilitates the efficient flow of
resources from nature to people back to nature. Within this
local chain, packaging, transportation, refrigeration, and all
other human activities that release CO_2 emissions are reduced to
a bare minimum. As Helena Norberg-Hodge said, localization
is the solution for healing our planet and people because it
'provides the economic structures that regenerate the fabric of
interdependence, promoting daily contact with others and with
the plants and animals in the natural world around us.' It is the
key to sustaining life itself.

Armed with a few gloves and sickles, we assisted Arii-san
for an hour of weeding and harvesting of mountain vegetables
from her farm. Our amicable conversations carried on as we put
our hands to work. The local kids gleefully joined us in this last
activity. They were pretty darn fast, I must admit.

Gurmet stood up and gave himself a stretch. 'Ah, this reminds
me of home. Back in Phyang village, we grow our own wheat and
barley. I used to work on the farm every summer with my parents
and grandparents. It was a bonding experience for the whole
family as we chit-chatted and sang to the mountains.'

'Let's go back to *memeley*'s farm next summer!' I replied and dug my fingers into the soil, pulling out a stubborn weed from the land. Its brawny roots were still clinging on to a bunch of soil. Close up an earthworm unveiled itself—dangling and wiggling. I carefully returned the worm to the ground and covered it with a patch of soil. 'There you go buddy, keep this soil alive.' This little being too is part of our family.

Author, Osamu, and Stanzin Gurmet taking a photo with Arii and the
kids at Shimosato.
Photo taken by Stanzin Angmo.

Chapter Eleven

無爲而農

Zen and the 'Do-Nothing' *Wuwei* Farmer

'Studying leads to daily increment [of knowledge]
The pursuit of Dao
leads to daily subtraction [of biases and excesses]
Subtract and simplify!
To the point of effortless actions (*wuwei*)
One acts without exertion,
Yet nothing goes undone.'

—Laozi[1]

Speaking of the Taiji-Daoist idea of 'moving a thousand pounds with four ounces,' I later found out that 530 miles southwest of Shimosato Farm, on the island of Shikoku, the philosopher-farmer Fukuoka Masanobu had taken farming to a whole new level by practising an even more esoteric and counter-intuitive method: one that requires *nothingness*. No plowing or tilling, no machinery, no pesticides or fertilizers, no cultivation, not even compost! All he had to do was to scatter seeds with the right

---

[1] 「為學日益， 為道日損。損之又損， 以至於無為。無為而無不為。」《老子》

method in the right season, practise a teeny-weeny bit of weeding, and then sit in idleness for the rest of his time. Yet, surprisingly, with each passing year, his soil grew richer, and his annual yield was comparable, if not greater than some of the most productive farms in Japan. Fukuoka called this method the 'natural farming of nothingness' (無の自然農法).

Trained as a plant pathologist, Fukuoka had a near-death experience in his early twenties followed by a spiritual epiphany that could best be described in Zen terminology as 'sudden awakening' (*dunwu* 頓悟). To give you a context, the sixth Zen patriarch, Huineng, from the seventh–eighth century, once had a similar awakening when he overheard someone reciting the Diamond Sutra verse 'to sustain one's heart without abiding in anything.'[2] After becoming a monk, Huineng's teacher Hongren one day instructed them to compose a poem to test their understanding of the dharma. In the middle of the night, his senior brother, Shenxiu, wrote on the wall:

身是菩提樹	The body is a Bodhi tree (perfect wisdom).
心如明鏡台	The mind is akin to a luminous mirror.
時時勤拂拭	From time to time, wipe it clean,
勿使惹塵埃	Let no dust settle on it.

The next morning, after having someone read to him the poem on the wall, the illiterate Huineng requested the person to help him write an alternative poem by its side:

菩提本無樹	The Bodhi originally has no trees
明鏡亦非台	The mirror has no stand
本來無一物	If in the beginning there was nothing
何處惹塵埃	How and where can dust ever contaminate?

Master Hongren was impressed when he saw Huineng's poem. The story goes that Hongren later passed on his dharma heir to

---

[2] From the Diamond Sutra: "應無所住而生其心"

Huineng instead of Shenxiu. But if indeed there was nothing in the beginning . . . why even bother writing? Hongren took off his shoe and wiped both poems off. Now, the wall is truly luminous. The Zen notion of emptiness is beyond words and letters, and of course, beyond the Zen tradition itself.

Masanobu Fukuoka's intuitive realization of emptiness was on an occasion triggered by the sharp cry of a night heron flapping its wings in the near distance when he was half asleep under a tree overlooking the harbour. In that instance, his doubts, confusion, and notion of 'self' faded away. 'My spirit became light and clear. I was dancing wildly for joy . . . Without thinking about them, words came from my mouth: "In this world there is *nothing* at all . . ."' Fukuoka wrote in his memoir. The next day, he immediately quit his job, wandered around the country for a bit, then returned home to his dad's farm, eager to put his realization to test. The philosophy of nothingness, he thought, need not be expressed and conveyed through convoluted Zen koans, nor must it be attained through long hours of zazen meditation. To Fukuoka, one should be able to penetrate it via the most mundane yet simple and serviceable livelihood—the Dao of Farming.

Trusting that humans should not interfere with Nature, Fukuoka first left his dad's meticulously pruned citrus orchard to its own. Not long after, branches became tangled, insects attacked, and hundreds of trees were decimated. Well, sudden awakening doesn't equate to being omniscient! Fukuoka's first test of 'doing nothing' failed miserably. Nonetheless, it taught him an important lesson on the difference between true *wuwei* and abandonment—you can't expect Nature to function regeneratively in an environment that is hitherto damaged and altered by human behaviour. Despite the setback, Fukuoka's glimpse into his 'true nature' was so potent that his faith never wavered. For the rest of his life, he directed his mind towards studying Nature.

When the Second World War broke out, Fukuoka did a short stint to work as the Head Researcher of Disease and Insect Control for Kochi Prefecture during which he researched scientific agriculture and pondered the relationship between chemical and natural farming. Once the war ended, he returned to his family farm and spent the next thirty years of his life in relative isolation. From time to time, he would take long walks into the wild, emptying his mind and simply absorbing what he could from nature. He noticed how human farms and orchards were often monoculture and consisted of very few specialized crops; while nature in its own course was abundant, multicultural, and biodiverse. The soil in human farmland tended to erode and deplete over time, but soil fertility in the forests increased with the natural accumulation of organic remains as proven by the growth of tall gigantic trees without the need of any fertilizers. In human farms, plowing and herbicides were constantly needed because weeds were growing out of control and competing with crops for nutrients; but in the wild, they were naturally regulated and coexisted with other plant species without causing any problems. Fukuoka began questioning many of the established practices of modern agriculture, 'How about NOT doing this or that? What is the natural pattern?'

Fukuoka Masanobu in his natural farm.
Photo courtesy of Masanobu Fukuoka Natural Farm.

松 Embodying Nature's *Song*

Upon returning to his orchard, Fukuoka attempted various experiments with farming by emulating Nature as closely as possible. The esoteric principles in agriculture—parallel to the deconditioning of bad mental and physical habits in Taijiquan and other contemplative studies—requires first and foremost the removal of brute force or unsustainable practices to embody a quality of *song* 松. Like blockages in the human body, soil in fields become compacted and hard when they are exhausted and deficient in oxygen. To loosen up soil in the deep strata, Fukuoka first planted fast-growing, nitrogen-fixing acacia trees and 'scattered seeds of deep-rooting vegetables such as dandelion, burdock, dock, and daikon radish'.[3] These plants help to open up channels for air and water circulation. The growth of acacia trees and other varieties simultaneously attract bees with their flowers and sustain the habitat of many natural predators such as ladybugs. Then Fukuoka sowed a mixture of hardy plants with fibrous roots such as buckwheat, mustard, turnip, amaranth, and yarrow to loosen up the topsoil; and finally, he covered the surface ground with white clover, vetch, and alfalfa that nourish the soil and suppress weeds.

As the soil comes to life, so does the rich biodiversity in the orchard. Microorganisms, plants, and animals become part of an endless cycle of life and death that continuously adds on to the organic matter and fertility of the soil. 'With tall trees for windbreaks, citrus in the middle, and a green manure cover below, I have found a way to take it easy and let the orchard manage itself,' Fukuoka wrote.[4] To an outsider, his orchard may have seemed chaotic and haphazard but there was actually a

---

[3] Larry Korn, *One-Straw Revolutionary: The Philosophy and Work of Masanobu Fukuoka* (Vermont: Chelsea Green Publishing, 2015).

[4] Masanobu Fukuoka, *The One-Straw Revolution: An Introduction to Natural Farming.* New York Review Books Classics. (New York: New York Review Books, 2009).

hidden order within the chaos that only he had come to perceive and understand.

流 Allowing Nature to Flow

Once Fukuoka's orchard had been restored to a state of being resembling that of a natural woodland or the Bulang's tea forests in Yunnan, natural resources flowed on their own like moving clouds and flowing rivers. Nature is circulating and humans can take whatever they need from this stream of abundance as long as they don't disrupt the balance of nature through extreme activity such as over-extraction, pollution, or altering the natural biosphere. All Fukuoka did at his orchard was to randomly scatter seeds of fruits, berries, nut-bearing trees, and other plants periodically and moderately harvest the yield when they were ready without needing to prune, fertilize, or apply herbicides or insecticides.

Building on this principle of intuitive grasping and embodying nature's pattern, Fukuoka continued to refine his flow of *nothingness* in the field of agriculture and channel it towards his grain fields. There, he developed an interesting sequence of crop rotation that was in harmony with the seasons and terrain of his local environment (heaven and earth), and for himself (humans). Winter rye, barley seeds, and clover were broadcasted in the fall even before the ripening stalks of rice were harvested; and similarly rice seeding was performed either in the late fall directly into growing young barley plants, or in the spring two weeks before the winter crop matured. By doing so, the soil actually became enriched over time.

But there was one important skilful means or *shi* 勢[5] that Fukuoka discovered, which made this flow or succession possible without needing to plow, transplant, weed, irrigate, or fertilize his

---

[5] skilful means, strategic advantage, or propensity

grain field. He called it the *One Straw Revolution*—the title of his first book. Besides seeding at the right timing, the uncut straws of rice, rye, and barley needed to be returned to the fields right after harvest and be randomly tossed around as though they had fallen naturally to the ground. These scattered straws alongside the white clover not only helped to maintain the soil structure by decomposing into natural fertilizers, but also aided in suppressing the growth of weeds.

Fukuoka Masanobu speaking on the One Straw Revolution.
Photo courtesy of Teruo Ootomo.

'My fields may be the only ones in Japan, which have not been plowed for over twenty years, and the quality of the soil improves with each season. I would estimate that the surface layer, rich in humus, has become enriched to a depth of more than four inches during these years. This is largely the result of returning to the soil everything grown in the field but the grain itself.'

治 Regulating Nature's Flow & Reviving Global Harmony

Having remodelled his farms to embody the pattern of nature and flow, Fukuoka only needed to add in a tiny effort to regulate and maintain this state of harmony through direct seeding in a simple and creative way. He mixed various kinds of seeds of native trees, fruits, vegetables, clover, and medicinal herbs with water and moist clay, then kneaded them into 'seed balls' or 'clay seed pellets' (*nendo tango* 粘土団子). Similar to the way he spread grain straws, he simply cast these seed balls arbitrarily around his farm and waited for them to germinate on their own. Since there are many different types of seeds within a pellet, some will prosper, others won't. But the ones that grow, will grow well because they are suited to their environment and climate, and thus will continue to flourish without the help of human beings. Fukuoka said in an interview, 'when you plan and dictate where plants should or should not be planted, you won't end up with big discoveries. But with this method, you might be surprised to find a burdock root growing happily in an unexpected place. Just plant diversity in a random manner and wait for nature to reveal what's best for it.'[6] One finds an interesting passage from *Laozi* that explains Fukuoka's Dao of Farming:

> Because sages act in *wuwei* – effortlessly without forcing anything thus, nothing is ruined.
> Without having any attachment,

[6] From NHK 総合・津 NHK 映像ファイル あの人に会いたい「福岡正信（自然農法家）」2011/06/01

nothing is lost.

Most people tend to fail

just on the very brink of materialization.

Therefore, if one can maintain a beginner's mind through the end,

He or she is free of failure.

It is for this reason that sages seek to detach from desires.

To not be attached with properties or goods that are hard
to come by.

They learn through unlearning

And by revisiting the mistakes of others.

They assist myriad beings to develop naturally according to
their own course (*ziran*自然)

without forceful interference.[7]

Fukuoka's 'natural farming of nothingness' is a classic example
of assisting plants, animals, microorganisms, and soil to develop
naturally according to their own course without forceful
interference. When humans' discriminating mind places us as
outsiders, or as superior to nature, we tend to want to control
the outcomes of nature, and thus deviate further away from the
Dao. Our actions wind up as a form of interference. However,
Fukuoka's way of seedling, for instance, bears a resemblance to
the dispersal of seeds by animals in the wild. Accepting human
ignorance and keeping a beginner's mind, he surrendered to
nature and subtly blended himself as part of its cycle.

After Fukuoka's Japanese and English edition of the *One
Straw Revolution* came out in the 1970s, his work became well-
known internationally and he began to travel extensively around
the world to share his philosophy and practices with other local

---

[7] 「是以聖人無為也，故無敗也；無執也，故無失也。民之從事也，恆
於其成事而敗之。故慎終若始，則無敗事矣。是以聖人慾不欲，不貴
難得之貨；學不學，而復眾人之所過；能輔萬物之自然，而弗敢為。
」《长沙马王堆帛书老子甲乙本合订校订本》

communities. Elsewhere, he proved that the spirit of natural farming—of simplicity and trust in nature's wisdom—endures, but techniques may vary due to differences in local topography, climate, and native species. Another thing that struck Fukuoka during his travels abroad was witnessing the intensity of desertification in many countries caused by human activity. This agitated him to do something to restore the earth, as he came to the realization that rain does not spring out of nowhere from the clouds in the sky, it actually comes from greenery.[8] 'Originally, water, soil, and crops were a single unit, but since the time people came to distinguish soil from water, and to separate soil from crops, the links among the three were broken.' Fukuoka wrote in his last major work, *Sowing Seeds in the Desert*.

For the final thirty years of his life, Fukuoka dedicated most of his time and effort to developing, organizing, and propagating broad-scale aerial seeding based on his same approach of natural farming to counter desertification in places like America, India, and Africa. In the year 2008, at the age of ninety-five, Fukuoka passed away peacefully at his home in Iyo, Ehime Prefecture, bearing hope that his *yoin* 余韻—legacy and spirit of nothingness will flow on into the future of humanity.

Sudden Awakening vs Gradualism

Let us take a moment to revisit the Zen verses of Huineng and Shenxiu in the beginning of the chapter. For centuries, Shenxiu's poem and his teachings have often been regarded as a gradualist approach compared to Huineng's subitism[9], and sometimes

---

[8] 「雨は緑から降るんだ。水から出来るんだ。空の雲から湧くんじゃない」ということを言いおったのが、いよいよそういうことを真剣に考え出すんですよ。From NHK documentary.

[9] The word *subitism* means 'sudden awakening'.

attacked as being inferior. I would say that Fukuoka's philosophy
and way of life transcends the duality of Huineng and Shenxiu: his
epiphany of nothingness early in his life mirrors that of Huineng's
sudden awakening, but his 'Dao of Farming' provides an alternative
interpretation and a deeper appreciation for Shenxiu's verses.

身是菩提樹   The body is a Bodhi tree (perfect wisdom).
心如明鏡台   The mind is akin to a luminous mirror.
時時勤拂拭   From time to time, wipe it clean,
勿使惹塵埃   Let no dust settle on it.

One way of interpreting Shenxiu's poem is that the first two
lines of the poem literally represent the first esoteric principle
of this book, which is to allow our body, or in Fukuoka's case,
the soil to embody a state of natural *song* 松 that is analogous
to that of a Bodhi tree or natural pattern; as well as to cultivate
a non-discriminating mind that reflects the true nature of all
phenomenon like a mirror. A mirror does not react nor desire to
control, but simply reflects and provides observation. The third
line of 'wiping it clean' could reflect the second esoteric principle
of flow, which requires good pacing, and an effortless mastery
of skilful means. One's act of wiping need not be forceful and
arduous, but done so in a gentle and relaxing manner without
exerting brute force. In fact, during the Buddha's time, the absent-
minded disciple Ksudrapanthaka was able to gain enlightenment
just by constantly repeating the phrase 'sweep and clean' while
sweeping the ground and one day realizing the great wisdom of
emptiness when his dirt of human greed, anger, and ignorance
was cleansed. Finally, the third and fourth line of the verse is
compatible with the third esoteric principle of regulation and
maintenance. Even after restoring his orchard and grain fields to
resemble that of a natural woodland and natural grassland, 'from

time to time,' with the right degree (*du* 度),[10] Fukuoka still had to put in some effort in sowing the seeds and spreading the straw to keep them in a state of harmony. As the late *chan* (Zen) master Sheng Yen put it, '"Theories, truth, order, or metapatterns" (*li* 理) have to be realized intuitively, but "specific matter or things" (*shi* 事) need to be cultivated gradually.'[11]

Fukuoka Masanobu, the philosopher-farmer.
Photo courtesy of Masanobu Fukuoka Natural Farm.

Haney Test: Gradualism and *Shi* (勢)

Keeping the importance of gradualism in mind, as exemplified by the steps taken by Shimosato and Fukuoka, it is also worth mentioning that one of the shared strategic advantages (*shi* 勢)

---

[10] *Du* 度 'degree or optimum measure', is a concept we will revisit and expand in the next chapter.

[11] 「理以頓悟，事以漸修」

that both farms have in aiding the transition towards organic and natural farming is their shared location of being close to the natural mountains. Kaneko's Shimosato Farm is located in a basin surrounded by mountains known as the Outer Chichibu. Just a short walk away from Shimosato, one stumbles upon a river flowing with crystal clear water connected to their irrigation canals. Fukuoka also recommends starting a natural farm in mountain foothills that are 'rich with the bounties of nature,' ideally close to a river. In this way, the rich humus, nutrients, and even bugs from the forest are naturally carried down into the farm from the slopes to assist in the reversal of chemical agriculture and in the development of natural farming. However, for the many farmers around the world without Fukuoka's deep intuitive understanding of nature and the geographical advantages of Shimosato, what is the first step that they could take? Is there another skilful means or propensity (*shi* 勢) to aid in the gradual transition towards natural farming?

As I continued to travel down this rabbit hole for an answer, I chanced upon the work of Dr Rick Haney, a researcher who had been travelling around the United States to resuscitate soil vitality by helping farmers better understand their soil and using progressive steps to cut back on their fertilizers. The Haney Test, which he developed, came about through an epiphany— he realized that soil is actually alive—during his time at graduate school that echoes the Japanese phrase *ikasu* 活かす. Microbes in soil take in oxygen and release carbon dioxide just like humans do. Keeping this perspective throughout his decades of research, Haney's test today has evolved to integrate information from as many instruments as possible to try and paint a more holistic picture of how microbially active or how alive one's soil is by determining the soil respiration rate, organic matter available, water-soluble organic carbon and organic nitrogen, as well as other chemical compounds in a sample.

Haney admits that it is mind-bogglingly complex to fully understand the soil as a dynamic living system. The Haney Test is an attempt to approximate Nature's pattern, such as simulating a plant root's interaction with the soil using naturally occurring organic acids, and alongside other data collected, provide a soil health score to farmers so that they can compare their field's soil with itself over time or with other sites that employ a different farming methodology. In this way, scientists and farmers can start a conversation with their soil and see how it reacts to management change. 'This is not my test. This is Nature's test,' Haney humbly refused the credit and recognition people gave him. In fact, when he first created the test, he named the test as 'the soil health nutrient tool', but later on people started associating the test with his name. 'My job is to try and mimic nature in the field because all the lab and what we've been doing up until now is like let's get the soil in the lab and beat it up with whatever we think we should do. [The Haney Test] is more of a test that asks your soil, what we can do to help it.'

Half a century practice of chemical agriculture not only led to soil erosion but caused many farmers to become 'technologically locked in' to unsustainable practices. Capitalism and its model of maximizing profit and incentivizing competition further pushed agricultural prices down and stripped farmers of any control over commodities, seed cost, and equipment cost. As mentioned in our earlier chapters, it is not easy for farmers to just give up on chemical inputs and still thrive financially in the short run. Nevertheless, there is one thing that is still within their grasp, Haney observed, and that is having the decision over how much fertilizers they apply, which could serve as an opening move, a *shi* towards full regeneration. By showing farmers the aliveness of soil and how it is capable of supplying inherent nitrogen, phosphorus, and potassium on its own, the Haney test at the very outset, intends to convince farmers on cutting back on fertilizers so that they can save money, improve their soil health, and yet sustain yield. But beyond that, it has proved extremely effective in assisting the gradual implementation of natural methods such as those advocated by Fukuoka, for instance cover crops, no-tillage, crop diversification, and biological pest controls in easing the transition towards natural farming.

'Our job is to give farmers the confidence to make these changes. We say, "Try this out on 100 acres. I'm not saying do this on all your 2,000 acres. Use baby steps. And if it works for you, adopt it." We've had guys who tell me, "You saved me $60,000 in fertilizer costs last year."' Haney said in an interview with Yale Environment 360.

With the help of the Haney test, many farmers have successfully converted their farms from conventional farming to regenerative agriculture. The award-winning first-generation farmer Russel Hedrick from North Carolina was able to reduce fertilizer inputs on his cash crops and further implemented multi-species cover crops alongside cattle mob-grazing on his 800-acre field, saving himself thousands of dollars while increasing productivity. Indiana farmer Rick Clark transformed his 7,000-acre farmland to 100 per cent non-GMO, 100 per cent no-till, and 100 per cent cover crop, and on top of that, dedicated a third of his farmland to no-till organic farming.[12] Mitchell and Brian Hora, a pair of father and son farmers in Iowa, not only converted their own farms to a no-till cover crop, but are still running on-farm research and educational work, using the Haney test to share their insights and data on ways to improve soil health and water quality. Their bigger mission is to scale these regenerative practices to a wider audience through consulting and have provided consultation for more than 120,000 acres of farms nationwide.

---

[12] Field Work Talk Podcast, 'Rick Haney's Uncommon Sense', Published on June 15, 2021, https://www.fieldworktalk.org/episode/2021/06/16/rick-haneys-uncommon-sense.

Perhaps we can call this the start of the Haney Test Revolution, which shares a common root with Fukuoka's One-Straw Revolution—both stem from a spirit of trusting and respecting nature, working with nature and becoming part of nature instead of trying to control or fight it. The Haney Test is compelling because it speaks to lay people, and especially to farmers in a language of science and familiarity that they have become accustomed to. Even though Fukuoka derived his methodology from pure intuitive wisdom, and was often critical of scientists because he saw the massive destruction caused by science and its peril of often seeing objects in isolation from the whole, I see the Haney test as an outlier and a breakthrough within science to try and integrate its findings within the context of an ever-changing dynamic whole, and to accept human ignorance and its lack of comprehension. As Haney would put it, 'we are only at the tip of the iceberg in terms of what we understand about how soil functions and its biology.

All in all, the path towards effortless action (*wuwei* 無為) is built on the foundation of intentional 'cultivation and refinement' (*xiulian* 修煉)—a Daoist jargon used to describe the alchemical transformation of body–mind, one's actions, and myriad things through an endless process of integration (*hanhua* 涵化). Just as yoga and other forms of moving meditation can serve as an entrée into quiet sitting meditation, eco-efficiency—the strategy of doing more with less—is the entrée into sustainability and regeneration. But sometimes we just have to find the right skilful means (*shi* 勢) to propel change. For Google's pioneer Chade-Meng Tan, the first step to cultivating mindfulness starts with just committing to taking one mindful breath a day, or in his case sitting quietly and joyfully with his daughter for two minutes a day. For Fukuoka, it was planting deep-rooting nitrogen fixing trees to loosen up the soil. For Haney and many farmers in the US, it could be cutting back on fertilizers and planting clover. The key is to find the right methodology, jumpstart your vehicle, and preserve the momentum while you gradually make your way towards what Fukuoka would deem *nothingness*. Who knows, at any point along this journey, you might experience an intuitive understanding or a new awakening that transforms your whole being and outlook in life.

A quote by Jacob Riis, the Danish-American journalist who trailblazed the use of photography for social reforms, sums up the value of gradualism:

> Look at a stonecutter hammering away at his rock, perhaps a hundred times without as much as a crack showing in it. Yet at the hundred-and-first blow it will split in two, and I know it was not the last blow that did it, but all that had gone before.

The Dao of Flow would further suggest that the stonecutter embodies a state of cultivated relaxation and enjoyment, *song*, while doing the hammering and refines his actions such that they flow from one to the next naturally with harmonious pacing, all the while making sure that the end goal of 'splitting the rock' fits in with the bigger picture of serving the well-being of people and the planet.

Himalayan painting by Penangite artist Sim See San

Part IV

Shui 水

Be like Water

行 雲 流 水

Chapter Twelve

呂植

The Jane Goodall of China: From Panda-Shadowing to Biodiversity Conservation

'In the Age of Sublime Virtue, humans' actions were grounded, their gaze soft and far-reaching. In those times, there were no paths or tunnels through the mountains, no boats or bridges over bodies of water; Myriad beings lived together, their homeland connected. The birds and beasts banded together, and the grasses and trees grew luxuriant. Thus, one could tie a leash to an animal and playfully wander around with it; one could climb up trees and peep into a bird's nest without causing harm.'

—*Zhuangzi* [1]

When I first became an exchange student at Peking University, I was enthralled by the overwhelming beauty of its nature. Located among a lush canopy of green foliage, just north of the heart of the campus, *Weiminghu*, the lake without a name, spreads out in

---

[1] 「故至德之世，其行填填，其視顛顛。當是時也，山無蹊隧，澤無舟梁；萬物群生，連屬其鄉；禽獸成群，草木遂長。是故禽獸可係羈而遊，鳥鵲之巢可攀援而闚。」《莊子·外篇·馬蹄》

the shape of a fat coiled caterpillar, its shimmering skin reflects the blue sky and mirrors its surrounding flora and fauna. My favourite activity here was to circle around the lake on its walking trail, soothed by the songs of chirping birds and enlivened by the sight of quacking ducks and swans paddling across the surface. Peking University was clearly inhabited by more creatures and vegetation than any other campus I have visited, but little did I know that within this community of more than 50,000 students, faculty, and daily visitors, this 680-acre enclosed land is also home to:

- Over 620 plant species, most of which are native to Beijing itself. (This translates to about 2 per cent of total plant species found in China)
- Over 235 bird species (1/7 of total bird species in China)
- 11 species of mammals, 26 species of fish, 11 species of amphibians and reptiles, 27 species of butterflies, and 26 species of dragonflies
- Several first and second-class state-protected animals, such as the Yellow-breasted Bunting, Golden Eagle, Eurasian Sparrowhawk, Eurasian Scops Owl, and the Mandarin Duck.[2]

Map of Peking University. Weiminghu, the lake without a name, is located slightly towards the north of the campus heart. Source: PKU website.

---

[2] https://news.pku.edu.cn/xwzh/6a558aa51de941abb968eea92a2f5285.htm

Amidst the capital of the Middle Kingdom, a metropolis of twenty million, Peking University is a remarkable biodiversity hotspot in an urban setting. Its unique blend of rugged wilderness and historic architecture serves as a respite from the hustle and bustle of Beijing's city life, as well as a testament that nature and human endeavours could coexist.

In 2018, about a third of Peking University's land was designated as a campus nature reserve, making it one of the first of its kind in the nation. Each week, students from the Peking University Green Life Association take turns to birdwatch and conduct systematic observations and monitoring of various animals and plant phenology on the campus. They organize educational activities to spread awareness of conservation and participate in the management and maintenance of the campus' protected area, such as advising the school on its tree-cutting activity.

What was even more awe-inspiring, I found out, was that many of these conservation efforts were spearheaded by a female professor by the name of Lü Zhi 呂植 from the School of Life Sciences. Professor Lü (pronounced as 'leui') holds many prominent positions, including the executive director of Peking University's Center for Nature and Society, vice president of China Women's Association for Science and Technology, and an advisor to the UN's Decade on Ecosystem Restoration 2021–2030.

Above all, Lü Zhi is perhaps most famous in China as 'the lady dearest to Pandas.'

Lü Zhi's Embodiment of *Song*: The Dao of Panda Shadowing

Lü Zhi has been a *Beida-Ren*, a true community member of Peking University, since 1981. As an academic prodigy, she was enrolled in the School of Biology at the age of sixteen but slowly grew tired of the dry, mundane life of laboratory biology and chemistry by

her junior year. Life took a different turn when she met Professor
Pan Wenshi, China's leading panda expert, who was at that
time working with the WWF in setting up the Wolong National
Nature Reserve in Sichuan province. Professor Pan's storytelling
captivated her. In a discussion about the Dao of Flow that Lü Zhi
and I were having over a cup of tea, she told me:

> Girls are often limited by social norms. I want to defy that, and
> I wanted to do something different from my classmates. For
> me, the idea of *song* 松 is to have the flexibility and freedom to
> act with ease, as well as the ability to *she* 捨 (let go), to reduce
> human greed and discard negative constraints. In today's
> capitalistic society, we seem to be losing much of this quality.
> All my life, I felt like I was chosen to pursue this path. The only
> purposeful decision I had to make in life with conviction was
> to switch over to the zoology department so that I could study
> with Professor Pan. Since then, things unfolded naturally,
> flowing from one to another.

Under the tutelage of Pan Wenshi, Lü Zhi was quickly sent off to
the high-altitude forests of northwest China's Shaanxi Province
in 1985 to study the socio-ecological system and genetic diversity
of giant pandas in this region. People around her were dismissive
and doubtful, claiming that mountainous field work was too
physically demanding a job for a girl. 'But when I actually got
into the field, I didn't find any disadvantage. I was young, fit, and
I enjoyed climbing. In fact, I feel that women have the advantage
of patience to observe animal behaviour, and to better empathize
with others.' The mountains were beautiful, and the experience
was extremely liberating for Lü Zhi. Perhaps it was beginner's
luck, maybe it was a call from nature—within the first four days
of her field trip, Lü Zhi bumped into her first wild panda, an
incredible feat that usually took months for an amateur. She was
exhilarated.

Pan Wenshi and Lü Zhi tending to a baby panda.
Photo courtesy of Lü Zhi.

'The most difficult thing about researching wild pandas is that they run away when they see humans. It is their natural instinct.' Lü Zhi woke up every morning pondering and plotting different ways that might enable her to encounter a panda. 'What will pandas be doing today? Which paths should I take? How can I convey a sense of goodwill so that they wouldn't be afraid of me?' She learned to imitate their sounds and continued trailing pandas until finally winning the friendship of more than twenty wild pandas.

One year, Lü Zhi and her assistant were spending their spring festival in the wild when she came across a familiar male panda whom she had previously named Da Xiong, comfortably munching off some bamboo shoots nearby. It was a completely random encounter, so Lü Zhi gradually approached the panda, wanting to test out the bear's tolerance of her presence. Da Xiong froze when he noticed Lü Zhi. 'Because he'd seen me multiple times, he was confused whether or not to run away.'

When confronted with a wild animal, one should not show
any sign of threat nor weakness, but exude a calm but firm
demeanour, an embodiment of the quality of *song* 松. Lü Zhi
chose not to look at Da Xiong. She pretended to read her book
as naturally as she could while slowly pacing towards the bear
until she was about two metres away. Then she sat down right
next to him and continued reading. After some time, Da Xiong
started eating again, but every now and then, he would peek at
her. Lü's heart bounced and danced with every minute change in
Da Xiong's response.

> To a wild panda, human beings are a hostile threat. This is a
> consequence of how we humans have dealt with animals for
> millennia. But in that instance, I felt like I was able to transcend
> that boundary and just sit there as a friend. I read my book. He
> ate his bamboo. Such a harmonious and beautiful portrait of
> the natural world ought to have unfolded in eternity.

At another juncture, she helped an old giant panda remove a
piece of bamboo stuck in its loosening teeth and nursed it back
to health before freeing it back into the wild. The old panda
kept coming back to visit her until they had to anesthetize it and
send it deep into the forest. Perhaps Lü Zhi's most rewarding
experience was to habituate a mother panda, Jiao Jiao, to
her presence. Throughout their eight years of friendship,
Lü Zhi shadowed and documented in detail how she lived,
reproduced, and brought up her little cubs. She recalls entering
Jiao Jiao's den in August 1992 while she was still cradling and
breastfeeding her second cub. 'At first, she was a bit evasive.
She turned around and curled into a ball with her back facing
me. But when I gently placed my hand on her shoulder, she
didn't evade. And I knew at that moment that she'd accepted
me. It was extremely gratifying to know that we've developed
mutual trust after so many years.'

Lü Zhi's Flow into Conservation

'By maintaining unwavering oneness with the *du* 度 (optimum measure), the Dao accommodates and allows all kinds of creatures to co-exist – birds fly freely, fish swim with ease, and creatures run wild. Myriad beings depend on it to live; hundreds of affairs rely on it to be accomplished. Humans rely on it, not knowing its name. They use it, not seeing its forms.'

—*Huang-Lao Silk Text* [3]

Situated on the intersection of China's northern and southern domains, the Qinling Mountains are an ecological treasure trove that have witnessed and withstood countless human activity—from remnants of graphite, ancient mining shafts to traces of refuge-seeking commoners in times of war and famine. Throughout the ages, the mountains were in a constant tug-of-war between anthropogenic influences and natural regeneration. Yet each time, it was able to take a breather during gaps of human absence and heal itself back to an optimum state, thus continually providing people with various resources and synchronously sustaining a vast array of rare plants and wildlife animals, such as the golden snub-nosed monkeys, golden takins, and clouded leopards, not to mention the giant pandas.

On several occasions, Professor Lü Zhi brought up the subject of *du* 度. 'We have to figure out the range of *du* in each context—How much can we develop; how much should we preserve? And how do we find a balance between the two? Once we know the *du*, we have to practice self-restraint.' Professor Lü told me in our last meeting.

---

[3] 「一度不變，能適蚑蟯。鳥得而飛，魚得而游，獸得而走；萬物得之以生，百事得之以成。人皆以之，莫知其名。人皆用之，莫見其形。」《黃老帛書》

The Chinese character *du* 度 is an amalgamation of several meanings: degree, limitations, measurement, a sense of proportion, rule, to gauge, etc. But it could be best understood through the lens of moderation: the degree or magnitude of change that a system could tolerate in order for it to return to a harmonious equilibrium—an 'optimum measure' perhaps, as I would translate in the text above.

Lü Zhi's eight years of research in the Qinling Mountains coincided with the reform and opening up of China's economy, and she experienced first-hand the impact of that transition on the natural world. Despite Qinling Mountains' historical proof of resiliency, during that time, however, Lü Zhi was starting to worry about its innate ability to recover with the arrival of this new Anthropocene. The Qinling Mountains' state of *du* or 'optimum' was on the verge of collapse. In a conference on symbiosis with Berggruen Institute, Lü Zhi shared:

> When I first arrived, there was some form of logging in Qinling, but it was a planned economy. So logging was done moderately with the rule to retain at least 40% of forest canopy density. Trees regenerate and grow in abundance. However, with the introduction of a market economy in the early '90s, things started to change drastically. Companies were incentivized to cut down as many trees as possible to increase their profit. All of a sudden, we realized that the pandas were quickly losing their breeding ground.

Around this time, Panda Mama Jiao Jiao was already bearing her third child, and she was starting to feel the stress of deforestation. This observation triggered in Lü the urgency to protect animals. 'No one taught me the idea of conservation. It was an imperative need that grew out of my responsibility as a field researcher.'

Lü Zhi and her colleagues reached out to various governmental departments and wrote a letter to President Jiang Zemin and Premier Li Peng to express their apprehensions. Their voices reached the very top of the bureaucracy. Soon after, with financial aid from the World Bank, the government enforced a halt to deforestation by converting Qinling Mountains into nature reserves. For Lü Zhi and her team, it was a victorious moment, but she was not happy. 'The forestry laborers used to be very friendly to us. But overnight, they were losing their source of income. Even though they were offered about $5,500 to switch to another job, it was not voluntary. Many put up signs "forbidding scientific field research" where they were working as a subtle way of protesting against us.'

China was still a poor country then, and this was just the beginning of its decades-long development-oriented poverty alleviation. Many rural villages were still dependent on logging and the poaching of deer and other wild animals for their livelihood. In that instance, Lü Zhi realized that in order to make conservation work, they should focus not just on animals but also on social issues and human values. 'What are the relationships between individuals and nature? How can we finetune them? And how can we orchestrate the conditions for green transformation to take place?' Lü Zhi asked.

Conservation 'Propensities' (*Shi* 勢)

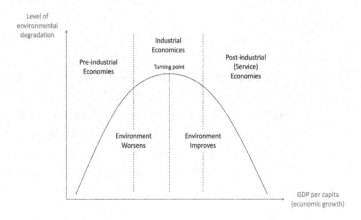

The Environmental Kuznets Curve

The Environmental Kuznets Curve (EKC) is often cited as an example of how economic growth could *eventually* lead to green transformation. The hypothesis, as demonstrated by many developed Western countries, suggests that in pre-industrial economies, nations rely on massive consumption of natural resources for their development, thus leading to greater environmental degradation. But once a nation develops into an industrial economy and reaches a certain level of GDP per capita (approx. $10,000), it hits a turning point. Investments are poured into cleaner, more efficient technology and the protection of the environment. Following that, the inverse becomes true, now economic growth is accompanied by a lower deterioration of the environment. Too good to be true?

Arguments built upon the EKC, such as 'we can't take care of these environmental problems *yet* because we are still at the rising curve of economic development,' are often used by developing countries in global negotiations to justify their carbon footprint. The EKC is a powerful empirical framework that invites deeper scrutiny:

1. The EKC may well be a fallacy. As high-income nations transitioned into a high-service economy, they merely exported their dirty industries and deforestation to lower-income nations.
2. The EKC may be true. But is time a commodity we can afford? If all nations were to follow this model, the earth's 'optimum' *might* crumble—hundreds of animals would go extinct, and maybe we might all be dead before the earth as a whole reaches Kuznek's turning point!
3. Regardless, there is some truth in the EKC: In order for conservation to work, we must first address the economic needs and social welfare of the local people around that ecosystem.

Lü Zhi understood the complexities of EKC and wanted to turn economic incentive into a driving force, a *shi* 勢 for catalyzing environmental protection. After conducting three-year-long postdoctoral research on the molecular genetics of wild giant pandas at the National Institutes of Health in the United States, she returned to China to work for the World Wildlife Fund (WWF). From 1995 to 2000, Lü Zhi successfully raised an annual budget of over US$1 million and focused not only on developing strategic plans and programmes for panda conservation but also the active promotion of eco-tourism in nature reserves as a means to develop the local economy.

> Ideally, ecotourism can help create a virtuous cycle of converting local people into conservation workers, but it is not easy to manage, for successful tourism brings about infrastructure growth to support the influx of people. So again, we have to figure out the *du*, optimum balance for development. Most importantly, we should keep in mind that the primary goal of ecotourism is conservation, not economics; and that whatever gain accrued should go toward the local community, not some foreign investors.

Under Lü's leadership, she helped to develop the Wanglang National Nature Reserve into an award-winning world-class ecotourism model by establishing facilities within the reserve, training local rangers who are highly competent and proud of their work, and engaging the local Baima ethnic communities to preserve and share their indigenous culture with the world. As a result, both the environment and the local people's livelihoods improved tremendously.

Lü Zhi doing fieldwork with Pan Wenshi and George Schaller.
Photo courtesy of Lü Zhi.

One of Lü Zhi's most influential mentors was George Schaller, the globe-trotting wildlife biologist who has researched many of the world's most iconic and endangered species—from mountain gorillas in Central Africa to tigers in India; from snow leopards and blue sheep in the Himalayas, jaguars and alligators in the Amazon forests to Asian Unicorns in Laos. Schaller was the first Westerner to study giant pandas in the Wolong Nature Reserve and the Qinling Mountains alongside Pan Wenshi in the early '80s, during which Lü Zhi became associated. 'I'm always amazed by Schaller's ability to navigate through different political regimes and cultures, and his single-minded dedication to studying one animal at a time,' Lü Zhi said. But perhaps Schaller's most remarkable feat, which he imparted to Lü Zhi, was to convert their research itself into a *shi* 勢 (a strategic advantage) and lobby for the whole world to protect not just one single species but the entire ecosystem that sustains it. Schaller's tactful diplomacy resulted in large stretches of forests and land areas around the world being designated as national reserves.

Pandas do not breed well in captivity, so in order to save them, the Chinese have to protect the pandas' natural habitat.

In China, as a result of Wolong and Qinling being converted into nature reserves, many other endangered species that were not as adorable as pandas also benefitted. 'It's a mystery why pandas evolved from carnivores into these bamboo-eating, black-and-white, cute-looking bears. Because they elicit the nurturing and protective instincts in us, they play the role of ambassadors for conservation,' Lü Zhi chuckled. As George Schaller once said: 'You can do the best science in the world, but unless emotion is involved, it's not really very relevant. Conservation is based on emotion. It comes from the heart, and one should never forget that.'

When Schaller and his wife received permits as the first foreigners to carry out field research in the remote Changtang region of Tibet, Lü Zhi tagged along. On the Qinghai–Tibetan plateau, she was introduced to a range of novel animal species, a fresh new ecosystem, and a mystical culture powered by a completely different set of values. A new paradigm shift occurred in her: Contrary to what the Environmental Kuznets Curve suggests, low-income societies can sometimes do a better job in conservation than high-income societies, as demonstrated by the Tibetan Buddhists.

The *Shi* 勢 (Strategic Advantage) of Sacred Mountains

Sanjiangyuan, the source of three rivers, is another natural biodiversity hotspot on the Qinghai–Tibetan plateau from where the headwaters of the Yellow, the Yangtze, and the Mekong Rivers originate. This elevated region comprises of an interconnected ecosystem of wetlands, grassland, and forests spanning a land mass of 363,000 square kilometres, roughly the size of Germany. In 2019, I made my first visit to parts of the Sanjiangyuan in Yushu, refreshed by the sight of thousands of yaks roaming across the green ocean, their herders moving along skilfully with their slings, always on the lookout for predators. On a drive to Nangchen, I witnessed a wolf killing and devouring a foal, a vulture on the lookout, and a local monk stopping by to say a few words of prayer. Here on the rooftop of the world, never was man apart from nature. Lü Zhi wrote:

> Our infrared cameras have captured images of the elusive snow leopards, brown bears, wolves, and lynx all roaming around the same area. The coexistence of multiple large carnivore species is a good indication of a holistic food chain. A snow leopard alone is sustained by a population of at least several hundred blue sheep, which in turn is sustained by a large grazing land.[4]

As of 2023, Sanjiangyuan is sparsely populated by around 600,000 indigenous people, most of whom are Tibetans. When Lü Zhi first arrived at the Sanjiangyuan more than two decades ago, she was impressed by the vast expanse of untouched wilderness but even more so by the *pro bono* conservation work driven by the locals on a grassroots level. Some of the trees in this region were more than six hundred years old, and wild animals were less afraid of humans.

'How many nature reserves do you have here?' she once asked the local director of forestry at Chamdo.

'We have fifty-six in total.'

'But there's only one nature reserve on the official list.' Lü Zhi was puzzled.

'Oh, that is the "official" one. But the other fifty-five are self-designated. They are all "sacred mountains", protected by our own people. And we support them.'

In my discussion with Professor Lü, I was reminded of my time at Nangchen. A lama told me that the mountain in front of their monastery was rich in *Cordyceps sinensis*, one of the most expensive fungi in the world used as herbal medicine.

---

[4] Lü, Zhi 呂植. "善治人与野生动物共存的可能 [The Possibility of Harmonious Coexistence between Humans and Wildlife]." 人与生物圈 [*Man and the Biosphere*], no. 5 (2018): 52–55.

However, locals are prohibited from harvesting them for commercial purposes. 'It is a sacred mountain dedicated to the Medicine Buddha; you may only collect some herbs for your own consumption if you're sick. On this land, killing is forbidden,' the lama said. From Professor Lü, I learned that hundreds, if not thousands of such sacred mountains and sacred lakes are spread out across the Himalayas—each functioning not only as sacred abodes of enlightened beings, but also as a refuge to wild plants and creatures.

Author with Tibetan friends in Nangchen, Yushu,
which is part of the Sanjiangyuan

The worship of sacred mountains in Tibetan culture predates the arrival of Buddhism and was further fortified by Buddhist teaching after it syncretized with the local shamanistic Bon religion. Tibetan Buddhism espouses that all sentient beings are equal and capable of reaching enlightenment, and thus practitioners should wish for and work towards the liberation of all beings from suffering. The belief in karma, or cause and effect, further deters people from harming other beings. 'Tibetan friends often laughed at our

classification of animals based on their levels of endangerment.'
Lü Zhi said. 'Don't all animals deserve equal protection? They
would sometimes ask me.'

In Sanjiangyuan, she discovered the powerful role cultural
values play in the art of conservation. Her team's investigation
into hundreds of sacred mountains revealed a direct correlation
between local indigenous tradition and greater biodiversity. 'We've
often wondered which would work best: laws that are based on
punishment, or economic incentives that are based on financial
rewards. The Buddhist system is different. It comes from the heart
of the people.'[5] Lü Zhi shared in an interview for the Pulitzer
Center. Since the earliest days, many monasteries and local villages
have worked hand in hand to keep their sacred mountains intact.
They conduct weekly patrols around the mountains, uncovering
snares and keeping illegal loggers and poachers at bay. Even though
the Tibetans were not wealthy, something else was powering
them to think about the well-being of other living beings and
to participate in conservation proactively. 'As conservationists,
I think there's much to learn from them, and we could leverage
on cultural traditions to make a difference.'

The Jane Goodall of China and the Art of Regulation

'Indeed, in the Age of Sublime Virtue, people lived in harmony
with the animals, and are equal to the myriad beings; how then
could one distinguish between that of a noble person and a
petty human being? They were all the same in unknowing, thus
straying not from their virtues; they were all the same in non-
craving, therefore always in a state of pure simplicity. It is in

---

[5] Lihong Shi and Gary Marcuse, 'The Science of Sacred Mountain:
An Extended Interview with Dr. Lü Zhi', *Pulitzer Center*, November 29,
2014, https://pulitzercenter.org/stories/science-sacred-mountain-extended-
interview-dr-lu-zhi.

this state of unadorned simplicity that people actualized their innate potential.'

—*Zhuangzi* [6]

While the British primatologist Jane Goodall was known for dedicating decades of her life tracking down and studying chimpanzees in Tanzania, Lü Zhi has done similar work in China, shadowing giant pandas on the Qinling Mountains, snow leopards in the Sanjiangyuan, and more recently, Bengal tigers in Medog County—the last county in China to become accessible by road only since 2013. 'Thanks to its primitive isolation, Medog is the only remaining place in China where we know Bengal Tigers still exist. And most recently we finally caught it in motion.' She showed me the footage of a Bengal Tiger leaping through the subtropical forests where her team had installed camera traps.

Both Jane Goodall and Lü Zhi began their journey with an intense passion for wanting to understand the behaviour of one single species, but their research soon grew into a deep insight into the interconnectedness of multi-species ecosystems and human activities, which led to a lifetime advocacy for biodiversity conservation. In 1991, Jane founded Roots & Shoots to empower youths to work on environmental, conservation, and humanitarian issues in their own communities. More than a decade later, Lü Zhi founded the Shan Shui Conservation Center, a 'Chinese NGO dedicated to species and ecosystem conservation to help resolve the problem of human and nature coexistence.'[7] Over the years, the two have become friends.

The name Shan Shui is derived from two characters— *shan* 山 (mountains) and *shui* 水 (water), the two elements that

---

[6] 「夫至德之世，同與禽獸居，族與萬物並，惡乎知君子小人哉！同乎無知，其德不離；同乎無欲，是謂素樸。素樸而民性得矣。」《莊子·外篇·馬蹄》

[7] From Shan Shui's website: http://en.shanshui.org/about/shanshui/

Chinese believe make up nature's original landscape. Shan Shui Conservation Center's logo features a composition of these two characters superimposed on a black and white background, signifying the unity of yin and yang, the coming together of human and nature, science and tradition, knowledge and practice (*zhixing heyi* 知行合一). Lü Zhi formed Shan Shui in 2007 because she thought there were two gaps they could fill. One is to guide community-based conservation outside of government protected areas, providing a medium to engage those who care about the environment and endangered animals; and two is to use and empower data information they collected as evidence to push for science-based conservation and policy change.

Today, Shan Shui Conservation Center is working closely with local Tibetans to connect their indigenous practices with the scientific community, policy-makers, and the outside world. For decades, Lü Zhi and her team have mapped out sacred sites across the region, and pushed for these sites to be incorporated into conservation. By bringing monasteries, local dwellers, and government officials to a multiparty discussion, Shan Shui pioneered the Conservation Concession Program—an initiative to give local communities formal authorization to protect their land and sacred mountains through signing formal agreements with nature reserves bureaus. Locals who participated in this program were provided satellite phones, environmental education on patrolling and wildlife monitoring, and some form of financial assistance. These efforts culminated with the establishment of Sanjiangyuan National Park in 2020, the largest reserve in China that encompasses a total area of 123,100 square kilometres inhabited by 70,000 herdsmen. Borrowing Shan Shui's model and assistance, the national park hires one local ranger from each nomadic family, creating about 17,000 jobs for the herdsmen. 'The park divides its income into three portions: 45 per cent goes to the host family, 45 per cent to the village collective, and 10 per cent towards a wildlife conflict insurance plan. This third pool of money is established to compensate herdsmen in the event of their livestock being killed by snow leopards or other wild carnivores.' Lü Zhi explained about the national park's financial model.

In Sichuan's Guanba Village, which serves as an essential corridor for endangered giant pandas in neighbouring reserves, Shan Shui provided scientific guidance and economic incentives to help villagers convert from illegal logging and poaching towards sustainable beekeeping and fishing. Heeding Shan Shui's advice, villagers set up a bee cooperative to harvest indigenous bee honey in farms located at least 3 kilometres away from their residential areas to avoid pollution and then collaborate with Beijing-based Bee Panda to market their honey to consumers. They also made concerted efforts to protect their surrounding rivers and were able to revive the number of native catfish. More recently, villagers have resumed fishing in a sustainable way, making sure that it is carried out within the *du*, the right optimum measure, and that profit is fairly distributed among all villagers who diligently participated in patrolling and guarding the environment. 'Guanba's honey sells for around 300 RMB per bottle. But this value encapsulates more than just the material value of honey itself—the effort of people's conservation and the value of clean air, water, forests, healthy bees, and wild pandas. Do you think it's too much?' Lü Zhi asked.

To Lü, there is no one-size-fits-all solution. She describes her approach as *yinshi lidao* 因勢利導—steering and guiding the flow of resources and methodology based on the unique advantage and propensities (*shi*) of each community. In the Qinling forests, it was lobbying to save the pandas and championing eco-tourism. In the Himalayan plateau, it was a respect for the sacred mountains and traditions. In Guanba village, it was beekeeping, and sustainable fishing. At Peking University, it was setting up an urban nature reserve. With solid research and resolution as rooted as the mountains, and her strategies as flexible and adaptive as the water, Lü Zhi continues to inspire countless youths and females to follow in her footsteps in the Dao of conservation.

'What is your future aspiration?' I asked Professor Lü before I left Beijing.

'I am looking for the next opportunity to grow and contribute. But ideally, I hope Shan Shui will become obsolete one day,' she replied. Her ultimate goal is to have humans within nature reach a state of harmonious regulation without needing her to act at all (*wuwei erzhi* 無為而治). 'The day Shan Shui is dissolved will be the day everyone becomes a conservationist.'

Author with Professor Lü at Shambhala Studio, Beijing

Chapter Thirteen

藝之道

The Dao of Art: Han Meilin's
Far-Wandering and Unfettered Playfulness

'There is a fish in the Northern Sea named Kun. Kun's grandness spans who knows how many thousands of miles. He transmutes into a bird named Peng, whose gigantic back stretches who knows how many thousands of miles. When he exuberantly takes off into the air, his wings are like clouds hanging above the sky. This bird moves along with the ocean's rhythm toward the Southern Sea – that is the Pool of Heaven.'

—'Wandering Far and Ease' chapter in *Zhuangzi*[1]

Under the sweltering summer heat, Han Meilin was sweating profusely and on the verge of collapsing. His legs trembling, hands manacled and tied to a bike rack. While he had not eaten a single thing for two days, his escorts were indulging themselves in steamed buns in front of him. No one dared to offer him a bite. After all, he was branded a traitor. To steer clear of any linkages

---

[1] 「北冥有魚，其名為鯤。鯤之大，不知其幾千里也。化而為鳥，其名為鵬。鵬之背，不知其幾千里也；怒而飛，其翼若垂天之雲。是鳥也，海運則將徙於南冥。南冥者，天池也。」《莊子・逍遙遊》

with him would be the safest choice, they thought. As Meilin crouched down by the roadside, he noticed flies surrounding crumbs of steamed buns dropped by a spoiled kid who ate only the fillings and threw away the skin. Instinctively, he lunged straight for the crumbs and gobbled them up. He couldn't care less about the surrounding onlookers—some were drawn by curiosity and sympathy, others by evil contempt and disgust. He needed to survive. He was too young and there was so much beauty in this world. He knew that within him lay a vast potential that spanned who knows how many thousands of miles. Like Kun, the enormous fish of vast expanse in *Zhuangzi*, Meilin was still shrouded in an ocean of suffering, waiting to embrace his metamorphosis and flight to freedom.

But this was just the beginning of a decade-long ordeal. Later on, he was put into labour reform at the Huainan Porcelain factory, then into prison, beaten, tortured, and humiliated. One persecutor broke his legs in an interrogation, another cut his hand tendon and destroyed his thumbs' mobility—perhaps the worst suffering one could inflict upon a painter. By then Meilin had completely lost faith in humanity. The closest people around him had not only abandoned him, but even created false evidence to frame him as a counter-revolutionary to protect themselves. Ironically, in the abyss of suffering furthest away from human touch, Meilin found a glimmer of warmth and solace in the company of a brown puppy whom he addressed by Hai Er 孩兒, meaning 'son'. While people in the forced-labour prison camp tried best to avoid contact with him, Hai Er would always come wagging its tail and join him for meals. The complexities of human politics meant nothing to Hai Er. A dog knew only to reciprocate kindness.

And so, with Hai Er, Han Meilin could whisper and share his deepest feelings and secrets without fear, just as he would generously share a portion of his scanty food rations. In fact, that was how their friendship was sparked: through a gesture of goodwill. Then onwards, Hai Er served as a trusted confidant, following him everywhere, withstanding the hot temperature inside the burning kiln by Meilin's side and tailing him to the train station. Once Hai Er started barking and chasing after the train when he saw Meilin departing, not knowing that he would only be gone for the day. During the peak of the Cultural Revolution, when Meilin was publicly shamed and assaulted in a denunciation rally on the streets, Hai Er appeared and pounced on Meilin, licking his wounds. Confused at why strangers were attacking Meilin, he barked and tried to shield him against them. But the poor dog was dealt with a heavy blow. He retreated among the crowd, whimpering in pain.

After Meilin was released, he went back to the factory to reunite with Hai Er, even buying some meat on the way as a treat for the dog. But Hai Er was nowhere to be found. 'He died two days after his spine was broken,' a worker told him.

'I will never forget Hai Er. He died for me,' Han Meilin said in an interview.

'He taught me that animals can be humans' true friends.'

Han Meilin's Embodiment

> 'When Peng the phoenix began his journey towards the Southern Sea, ripples of water were generated beyond three thousand miles. He spiraled up ninety thousand miles into the sky and continued his journey relentlessly with the aid of the summer wind.'
>
> —*Zhuangzi*[2]

Despite his passing, Hai Er continued to live on in Meilin's life. The seed of love he had sowed in Meilin during the darkest period of his time soon blossomed into an endless spring of artistic inspiration—animating an infinite number of endearing and exquisite animal artworks. Haier served as a *shi* 勢, a propensity

---

[2] 「鵬之徙於南冥也，水擊三千里，摶扶搖而上者九萬里，去以六月息者也。」《莊子・逍遙遊》

that catalyzed a turning point in Meilin's life. After resuming his
career as an artist, Meilin channelled the saudade he felt for Hai
Er in his painting 'My Little Friend in Need' (1979)[3], an adorable
sketch of the puppy that was unveiled in his first art exhibition as
a tribute to his best friend. The audience was mesmerized by the
bright-eyed and bushy-tailed puppy. In his painting, they could
feel Han Meilin's strong optimism for life and his appreciation
of friendship that transcended anthropocentrism. Such qualities
were equally transmitted to his designs of other animals, such as
pandas, horses, oxen, herons, owls, bears, fish, deer, and the list
goes on—all of which can be easily searchable on the internet.
The artistic ripples unleashed by Han Meilin quickly reverberated
across the world. That same year, he toured North America and
held solo exhibitions in more than twenty countries.

Art must be masterful in three ways: techniques, aesthetics,
and spirit. In creating art, Han Meilin employs various tools—
pens, brushes, ink sticks, colour paints, some of which he devised
himself to achieve the aesthetics he desired. 'Paths are made by
walking,' Meilin asserts, 'in art, the end is what justifies its means.'
His art, sometimes compared to Picasso's, is known for the
unconventional use of basic geometrical shapes (squares, circles,
and triangles) to compose intricate designs. He would sometimes
exaggerate or accentuate certain body parts of an animal, such as
the eyes or face to evoke specific emotions or comical impressions.
His strokes are minimal yet substantial, striking yet relaxed (*song*
松)—a testament of his life-long refinement in skills of painting,
calligraphy, sculpture, and pottery. Some of this foundational
knowledge was first acquired at the Chinese Central Academy of
Arts & Design[4] during his younger days.

As Mihaly Csikszentmihalyi wrote in *Creativity: Flow and
the Psychology of Discovery and Invention*, 'A genuinely creative
accomplishment is almost never the result of a sudden insight,

---

[3] 「患难小友」
[4] 中央工艺美术学院

a light bulb flashing on in the dark, but comes after years of hard work.' This involves learning and assimilating the methods and styles of predecessors, discovering novelty, and making a creative contribution that would be appreciated by an audience. Put together, Meilin is adept in bringing out the *yun* 韻—the spirit that epitomizes each character's unique personality in an elegant and harmonious way. Art connoisseurs could almost immediately discern Han Meilin's work of art, not merely from his personal seal, but through the presence of his *yun*—an embedded spiritual trademark.

Han Meilin's painting of oxen and his sculpture of mother tending to a baby at the Han Meilin Art Musuem, Photo courtesy of Sasha Yang.

'It's one word. Love. The greatest love in this world is motherly love,'[5] Han Meilin explained the underlying spirit of his art. Having lost his father at the age of two, Meilin and his two siblings

---

5 「一个字， 爱。人间最伟大的爱就是母爱， 植物会用坚硬的外壳保护自己的种子、动物想尽各种方法庇护自己的幼崽， 人类的母爱更不胜枚举， 作为艺术家我就必须表达和歌颂这伟大的母爱。我常常会跟大自然、跟动物、跟我画的动物说话。因为我把它们都当成小孩儿， 我感觉我用母爱去对待它们， 这和我的人生经历有关。不管小猫小狗、还是小鼠小蛇， 无论小熊猫小狗熊、还是小狐狸猫头鹰， 我统

were single-handedly brought up by his mother. Thus, he felt a calling to embody and channel this emotion within his artwork. 'I often talk to nature, to animals, and especially to the animals I paint. I feel that I shower them with motherly love, which is related to my own life experience . . . Love is understood through hardship. When I returned from labor camps to the actual human world, a deep passion sprung from within—the impulse to love and appreciate everything in life.[6] Whether it's a kitten, puppy, a small mouse, snake, panda, fox, or an owl, I treat them all as my children, it's as simple as that.'

So, like a mother tending gently to her newborn, Meilin seeks to foster only the genuineness, goodness, and beauty in his creations. One cannot help but compare Han Meilin's insights with the work of Austrian psychiatrist and holocaust survivor Victor Frankl, who amidst the ubiquity of brutality, came to the realization that 'salvation of man is through love and in love'. Love allows a person to see the essential traits, features, and potential in the beloved, and *enables* that potential to be actualized. In the same vein, Meilin realizes love within himself, in Hai Er, in his family, community, nation, and all his creative artwork.

Two Wings of a Phoenix: Han Meilin's Boundless Flow of Inspiration

> The cicada and the pigeon laugh at Peng, saying, "We scurry up into the air, leaping from the elm to the sandalwood tree, and when we don't quite make it we just plummet to the ground.

统把他们当做孩子，就这么简单。」 http://www.hanmeilin.com/news_content.php?id=756

[6] 「我认为，只有从坎坷的生活里走出来，才懂得爱。等我回到人间时，我有一种激情，我爱生活的一切。」

What's all this about ascending ninety thousand miles and heading south?

—Zhuangzi[7]

While love is the internal powerhouse of Meilin's art, just as a phoenix depends on its pair of wings to fly, his endeavours and success are further supported by two major sources of inspiration akin to the bountiful flow of waters along the Yellow and Yangtze rivers—the two great Mother rivers that have nourished and brought forth Sinic civilization since time immemorial. Han Meilin's stamina to soar, glide, and hover indefatigably high up in the blue sky is dependent upon what he calls his 'art caravan' (*da peng che* 大篷車), a four-decade long unbroken legacy of annual pilgrimages around the country to learn from the past and the peasants. This ongoing project was named after the 1971 Indian Bollywood blockbuster *Caravan*, which tells the story of a jovial group of gypsies performing everywhere they go while also building rapport with the lower social class—honouring their optimism and fearless integrity amidst hardship.

Han's First Wing: Ancient Art

Meilin's first source of inspiration comes from Chinese ancient art that dates from the prehistoric, neolithic, and bronze age periods up through the Han Dynasty. 'I don't go to popular tourist destinations. I travel to remote mountains, pristine forests, and arid deserts in search of desolate land where civilization once flourished, for I am interested in ancient cultural relics that stood the test of time.' He is especially captivated by petroglyphs, motifs, and symbols in rock paintings across the country, in particular those found in the Helan Mountains of Ningxia created 3,000 to 10,000 years ago. 'The sight of rock paintings imbues me with

---

[7] 「 蜩與學鳩笑之曰：我決起而飛，槍榆、枋，時則不至而控於地而已矣，奚以之九萬里而南為？」《莊子・逍遙遊》

creativity and excitement. It enables me to contemplate more deeply about contemporary art, and carve out a new world that integrates antiquity and modernity.'[8]

Lying at the confluence of northern nomadic tribes and sedentary farmers, the Helan mountain range contains thousands of images depicting shamanic symbols, human figures, and various animals such as bison, wild boar, horses, deer, goats, camels, tigers, and birds. Some of these arts were very realistic, others abstract. But they are all usually quite simple in design. These petroglyphs leave behind traces of early human civilization—stories of predecessors, their way of living, and the myriad beings that they once came into contact with. 'You see, my horses and cattle, for instance, (like the Helan rock drawings) are three-dimensional and devoid of hooves. When an animal is running in the wild, its hooves are invisible, dynamic and hidden behind the clouds, fog and earth. Sometimes our ancestors knew better how to draw!'

Han Meilin has also collected tens of thousands of mostly indecipherable logographs—some of the earliest forms of Chinese characters that were engraved on oracle bones, bronze vessels, and bamboo slips. These logographs predate the small seal scripts that were standardized under the Qin Dynasty, during which they became obsolete, many destroyed. Remnants that survived or were unearthed in more recent times have lost their meanings and functionality. While they may be subjects of interest to historians and epigraphists, they were often brushed aside by ordinary people. What use could they be?

Yet, for whatever reason, Han Meilin was naturally drawn towards these 'useless' mysterious characters that he found aesthetically pleasing. At the outset, he merely thought it was fun to collect, trace, and record them in his sketchbooks. However, on a trip to Hong

---

[8] 「看到岩画, 总有一种创作的激情, 让我对现代艺术的思考更为深沉。现代艺术的创作与古老的传统相结合, 才能走出一条全新的路。
」

Kong, Meilin showed his sketchbook to Qi Gong 啟功, a renowned
Chinese calligrapher, artist, and sinologist—and he was awestruck.

> People may regard them as illegible trash. How meritorious
> of you to set up a 'sanctuary' for keeping these forsaken
> logographs! Nonetheless, what you have now is merely a
> sourcebook. Not art. It would be wonderful if you, as an artist,
> with your strong calligraphy background, could 'write' them
> out as a form of art. Learn their patterns, and use them to
> nourish your own brushwork.[9]

Qi Gong's words of encouragement set into motion a massive
project to resurrect these millennium-old logographs. 'To be
inspired,' in its Latin origin *inspirare*, means 'to breathe upon or
blow into'[10] something. On one end, Meilin was literally inhaling
and internalizing various forms of logographs into his body of
work to energize his creative cells. At the same time, by drawing,
writing, and concocting them into compositions of art, he was
infusing life into these tiny symbols, the exact meanings of which
no one could be sure of.

In 2008, when he finished compiling his first collection of works
based on logographs, the thought of publishing them as a book
sprang to mind, but Meilin wasn't sure what to name it. He sought
advice from another mentor Ji Xianlin 季羨林, a senior professor
of linguistics, history, and paleography at Peking University, who
was then, it turned out, living out the final year of his life.

Ji wielded his brush and wrote him two bold characters:
天書 *Tianshu*, or heavenly script—this became the title of Meilin's

---

[9] 「这些古文字，很多人都认不得了，原来都是垃圾，你现在做了一件功德无量的事情，你这是在办文字'收容所'呀. 古文字都是描下来的，只能说是资料，不能说是艺术。你要是能写出来就好了，你是画家，又有书法底子，别人还真写不了。『看它形，养我画』」"

[10] 'Inspire', Online Etymology Dictionary, https://www.etymonline.com/search?q=inspire.

book. As the title connotes, Meilin's *Tianshu* is a collection of artworks based on texts that are hard to read or understand yet strangely mesmerizing and awe-inspiring, for this 'heavenly script' was venerated and carefully flowed back to humanity through an artist's magic touch.

Han Meilin's artistic creations based on rock art and *Tianshu* at the Han Meilin Art Musuem.
Photo courtesy of Sasha Yang.

Meilin's playful attitude towards *Tianshu* conveyed the essence of another archetypal Zhuangzi parable. In one of Huizi's complaints about the uselessness of a huge tree and a big vessel grown out of the seeds of a large calabash that he decided to smash to pieces, Zhuangzi was amused at his friend's 'clogged mind'. His reply was classic:

The difference is all in the way the thing is used . . . How is it that you never considered using your enormous vessel as a boat to drift happily throughout the lakes and rivers . . . Why didn't you consider planting the tree in an empty countryside, on a vast open plain, where you can loaf and wander by its side effortlessly. And feeling so free-spirited, one may even take a nap below it![11]

---

[11] 「則所用之異也。今子有五石之瓠，　何不慮以為大樽而浮乎江湖，而憂其瓠落無所容？。。。今子有大樹，患其無用，何不樹之於無何

As Zhuangzi and Han Meilin imply, most people are concerned only with what seems useful on the surface. True mastery of the Dao, however, allows one to freely transform what is useless into something useful—all the while enjoying and playing with the process! In Meilin's case, he continued to drift, wander, and have fun with his 'useless' collection of ancient patterns, extending the application of rock art and *Tianshu* as major themes in his paintings, bronze and iron sculptures, ceramics, *zisha* teapots, prints, textiles, and wood carvings. His effort culminated in a recent exhibition of more than 1,500 beautiful *Tianshu* artworks at the Beijing Palace Museum in 2021.

Han's Second Wing: Folk Art

If we group *Tianshu*, Helanshan's rock art, and other historical relics under the umbrella of ancient art, then Han Meilin's second 'wing' or source of inspiration is folk art. Since 1977, Meilin's art caravan has trailed along *Sanjiangyuan* 三江源, the headwaters of three great rivers of Asia—the Yellow, the Yangtze, and the Mekong—in search of intangible cultural heritages preserved by diverse ethnic groups in different regions across China. His art caravan has driven from the central plains of Shandong (Han Meilin's birthplace) to the northwest frontier of Shaanxi and Ningxia, gone up the Himalayan plateau to Qinghai and Tibet, penetrated into the southwest hinterland of Guizhou, the tropical forests of Yunnan, and the Jiangnan region south of the Yangtze River.

Meilin's art caravan expeditions take weeks or months, during which he and his students stop by scores of local villages to interact with the peasants and ask to participate in their making of folk art. Besides sketching and absorbing patterns of local design, they also learn varied techniques of paper-cutting, handmade pottery, flour figures, methods of dyeing, woodworking, tea processing,

---

有之鄉，廣莫之野，彷徨乎無為其側，逍遙乎寢臥其下？不夭斤斧，物無害者，無所可用，安所困苦哉！」《莊子・逍遙遊》

etc. Meilin believes in the power of the naked eye and emotional touch over theoretical books. Meilin wrote:

> Everything I have seen, the grassland, the plateau, the ditties and songs with high pitches, the sheep and neighing horses, dry wells and murky water, the local girls, children, senior citizens, and haggard folks; the joy, anger, sadness, pleasure, sourness, sweetness, bitterness, and spiciness I felt; in observing, drawing, talking, doing, grunting, conversing, pinching, scissoring . . . participating in gongs, operas, folk songs, dances, rock paintings, pottery, paper-cutting; and in meeting village chiefs, farmers, officials, secretaries, drivers . . . These experiences radically transformed my perception of reality, and reoriented my aesthetic taste for creation.[12]

Tsinghua students sharing their personal collection of
Han Meilin's art prints with the author.

---

12 「我所见到的一切: 草滩、高原、小曲、高亢、羊群、马嘶、枯井、涩水、姑娘、小伙、暮老、佝媪，　以及喜、怒、哀、乐、酸、甜、苦、辣、看、画、聊、做、哼、讲、捏、剪……还有锣鼓、戏曲、民歌、舞蹈、岩画、土陶、剪纸、村长、农夫、大官、小官、县长、秘书、司机……信不信由你，　下去以后，　这些概念会让你有翻天覆地的新认知，你会重新构建你创作的艺术典型。」

Folk art is usually colourful, straightforward, and free of rigid rules or affectedness. It is grown organically out of grassroots communities and is used to depict the ordinary life of peasants with their shared values, cultures, and ways of living. However, for a long period of China's history, folk art was often scorned in juxtaposition to literati art, namely poetry, calligraphy, and paintings that were pioneered by the educated class of the Tang and Song dynasties. Contrary to folk art, literati paintings were drawn using minimal colours, focused primarily on the dexterous play of black ink brushwork and white space to achieve balance and harmony—an aesthetic ideal and method influenced by the philosophy of Confucianism, Chan Buddhism (Zen), and especially Daoism. Art, according to the literati, should exemplify the Daoist-Chan qualities of simplicity, tranquility, non-attachment, and effortless flow in expressing self-cultivation, embodying an otherworldly *yun* 韻, 'spiritual essence'. Therefore, their paintings were often centered around unadulterated themes of nature such as mountain and river landscapes or flowers, birds, plums, orchids, bamboo, and chrysanthemums—pure elements that symbolize freedom and a transcendence of self and society.

Dwelling in the Fuchun Mountains (1350) by the Yuan dynasty Daoist painter Huang Gongwang. One of the author's favourite literati paintings. Image courtesy of The National Palace Musuem, Taipei.

There is a lot of depth and substance to literary art. In literati paintings, for example, a miniature human figure, if included at all, is humbly and subtly immersed within a tiny corner of the grand universe represented by mountains and rivers, signifying the oneness of heaven, earth, and humans. Unfortunately, once the defining forms of literati paintings became codified and were regarded as superior, too many elitists turned dogmatic and biased towards folk images and folk style paintings. This resulted in the artistic alienation of Chinese intellectuals from the richness of ordinary life, which is a key spiritual element of the cosmos. Such an attachment to a form of Daoist-inspired literati art paradoxically ran counter to the Daoist notion of non-duality itself, for the *Zhuangzi* has long cautioned people against falling into the trap of a 'discriminating mind' (*chengxin* 成心), which could impede a holistic understanding of others' perspectives.

A distinction no doubt exists between greatness and mediocrity, much like the contrast of Peng the great phoenix and the fledgling pigeon. But differences arise merely as a product of varying scale, aptitude, upbringing, conditioning, and circumstances. Each individual is of course an expression of their own humanity within their own context. 'Thus, the Sage does not proceed from [rightness or wrongness] but instead allows them to be illuminated by Nature, through accommodating varying circumstances (*yinshi* 因是).'[13]

Despite being a literati, a graduate from one of the finest art schools in China, Han Meilin was eager to break conventional literati standards to illuminate the value of folk arts through accommodating them within his repository of creative output, just as the vast ocean gracefully embraces the inflow of hundreds of rivers (*haina baichuan* 海納百川). On top of Chinese painting's classic black-and-white ink wash, he adopts the peasants' popular use of primary and contrasting colours such as rose red, emerald green, blue, yellow, and purple. Instead of mere landscapes, he incorporates animal totems, tribal patterns, and other motifs in his designs. As a result, Han Meilin's works bear semblance to folk art—they are down-to-earth, close to the people, and serve to fulfil utilitarian and ornamental purposes.

In the *Zhuangzi* it is said that:

---

[13] 「是以聖人不由，而照之于天，亦因是也。」《莊子・齊物論》

A fish in the well cannot be informed of the vast ocean, for it is confined to spatial boundaries. Summer worms cannot be informed of the winter ice, for they are limited by temporal boundaries. A distorted learner cannot be informed of the Dao, for they are restricted by knowledge boundaries.

As humans, what boundaries are we confined by? How can we rise above our preconceived notions and self-imposed limitations? Han Meilin's capacious ability to transcend geographical, temporal, and knowledge boundaries has led to the development of an artistic style that is unique and ever changing, yet always in resonance with the general public. With each passing year, Han Meilin's set of wings—ancient and folk art—grew bigger and stronger, allowing him to shoulder numerous mega-projects. Among them are the twelve zodiac stamps for China Post, the Five-Dragon Clock Tower for the Summer Olympic Games in Atlanta in 1996, the phoenix symbol of Air China's emblem, and the Fuwa good-luck mascots that trotted around the world during the 2008 Beijing Summer Olympics. Most, if not all, contained much borrowed wisdom from his art caravan missions. As a manifestation of the Dao, art ought to be ineffable and boundless.

Regulating Life Through Art

Heaven and earth possess vast beauties but they do not speak of them . . . The sage is able to trace the beauty of heaven and earth to 'make sense and actualize' (da 達) the metapatterns of myriad things.[14]

Today, as of 2024, Han Meilin is 88 and is still one of the most prominent living practitioners of contemporary art in China.

---

[14] 「天地有大美而不言，四時有明法而不議，萬物有成理而不說。聖人者，原天地之美而達萬物之理。是故至人無為，大聖不作，觀於天地之謂也。」《莊子・外篇・知北遊》

Each day, his procreative energy seems to flow in abundance as he spends four hours reading, two hours practicing calligraphy, and the rest of his time painting—sometimes even while holding his baby boy in one arm (a child he begat at the age of eighty-two)!

Once a year, Meilin is thrilled to hop on his art caravan and wander far and unfettered into a great many villages and townships in China and in other countries too, not only to seek new inspiration for art, but also novel ways to contribute to the local community. The Han Meilin Art Foundation, which he co-founded in 2013 with his wife, Zhou Jianping, is now funding close to a dozen elementary schools in some of the remotest regions of China. The foundation also provides art classes to children, scholarships for disadvantaged university students, and financial support to numerous non-profits, craftsmen, and folk artists who are striving to preserve their local intangible cultural heritage. The tagline of his foundation says: 'The ocean of art is boundless, let us share and appreciate one another's beauty!' (藝海無涯，美美與共). Han's altruism extends beyond China to places like Southeast Asia and Africa. In recognition of his long-term commitment to promoting peace, art, and education around the world, Han Meilin was designated UNESCO Artist for Peace in 2015.

In China, Han Meilin's art museums are established in four locations—Beijing, Hangzhou, Yinchuan, and Yixing—housing tens of thousands of his artworks. 'One of the best decisions Meilin and I made in our lives was to decide seventeen years ago to donate all his artworks to our country,'[15] said Zhou Jianping, who married Han twenty years ago. 'Because the lifeblood of Meilin's art is drawn from folk and ancient Chinese culture, he feels a strong imperative to pay it back to the people. We hope that by donating everything to the nation and making our museums free of charge,

---

[15] 「美林和我此生做得最正确的一件事，便是在十七年前决定将作品捐给国家。」周建萍说。

more people can have direct access to the profundity of Chinese civilization through his artwork.'[16] Having gone through a lifetime of rocky paths filled with bumps and potholes, Meilin found in Jianping a beautiful soulmate who shares his magnanimous heart and is a dedicated 'partner in crime' for shattering stuffy conventions. If Meilin is Peng, the large phoenix bird travelling south towards the Southern Oblivion, then Jianping is analogous to the gusty wind that supports his enormous flight towards doing all that he could.

Meilin often describes himself as an 'ox sent down by Heaven to work hard his entire life.' What then is he working for? Is it fame? Status? Wealth? Perhaps in Han Meilin, we can discern the apotheosis of Dao as manifested through art. The more an artist approaches the Dao, the more he pours his time and full energy into work, yet the more fun and effortless work becomes to him. In Meilin's case, he exhibits a kind of religious zeal for bringing forth beauty in everything and everyone he encounters, while at the same time being detached from them. In a love proposal to Jianping, he once presented her with a small drawing of a baby phoenix, only to surprise her in the next moment with a total of 179 mini drawings of various animals and motif designs—a number that is pronounced the same as *yi qi jiu* 一起久, which means 'together forever' in Chinese. In a burst of energy one morning, he swiftly drew eighty dissimilar horses, which he packed into a single stack as a gift for his close friend Feng Jicai, who was celebrating his birthday and was born in the year of the horse. Passion, warmth, and kindness radiates from Han wherever he goes. Whether it's coming into contact with his doctors or nurses in the hospital, a staff member, a driver, a child in the village, or

---

16 「他从民间、从中华文化中汲取养分，理所当然也要用艺术反哺人民。所以把作品留给人民，建成艺术馆免费对公众开放，让公众通过美林的作品来了解中华文化的博大精深，这是我和美林的共同愿望。」周建萍说道。

a random stranger, he is always generous to share his boundless
energy and time, often spontaneously through a piece of drawing.
Another quote from the inner chapters of *Zhuangzi* best concludes
Meilin's flow of the Dao:

> Effortless action without regard to fame,
> effortless action without cleverly seeking treasures,
> effortless action without regard to worldly affairs,
> effortless action without dogmatism.
> In this manner, one wholeheartedly embodies the endless and
> inexhaustible Dao,
> playfully roaming around without leaving his mark,
> actualizing what he received from Nature.
> Without being ostentatious, this is true emptiness.
> The Consummate Person uses his mind like a mirror,
> rejecting nothing, welcoming nothing,
> accommodating everything but not possessing anything.
> Thus he can make things wonderful (*sheng* 勝) without harm.[17]

Han Meilin's Dao of Art is not reserved only to a handful of
great artists. To embody, flow, and regulate genuineness, loving-
kindness, and beauty in one's life, to find harmony between
the yin and the yang, the colourful and the mundane, the ebb
and the flow, life itself is a piece of art that awaits our creativity
and appreciation. Peng, the phoenix, comes in infinite forms
and stories.

---

[17] 「無為名尸，無為謀府，無為事任，無為知主。體盡無窮，而遊無
朕，盡其所受於天，而無見得，亦虛而已。至人之用心若鏡，不將不
迎，應而不藏，故能勝物而不傷。」《莊子・應帝王》

Han Meilin's news article from author's collection.
Courtesy of Tsinghua students.

Chapter Fourteen

中村哲

The Nakamura Methodology

'The essence of humans is rooted in the earth;
the essence of the earth depends on appropriateness;
appropriateness is born out of the right timing;
the usefulness of right timing depends on the people;
the usefulness of the people depends on their strength,
the usefulness of strength depends on its proper allocation.
If one knows the conditions of the terrain, plants the right crop at
the appropriate time and seasons and optimally allocates human
resources for work, then wealth shall grow. With moderate
taxation, people shall become prosperous. If the people become
prosperous, they will understand shame. If they understand
shame, they will develop the moral conscience to obey rules and
not commit crimes. Once good order becomes a habit and laws
are not broken, you have secured the Dao of victory.'

—Huang-Lao Silk Text [1]

---

[1] 「人之本在地，地之本在宜，宜之生在時，時之用在民，民之用在力，力之用在節。知地宜，須時而樹，節民力以使，則財生，賦斂有度則民富，民富則有佴(恥)，有佴則號令成俗而刑伐不犯，號令成俗而刑伐不犯則守固戰勝之道也。」《黃老帛書》

'Given the choice of anyone in the world, whom would you want as a dinner guest?'

'Nakamura Tetsu.'

This answer popped up multiple times whenever I went through 'The 36 Questions That Lead to Love'—a set of prompts designed to help unlock vulnerability and build intimacy between partners.

I've always wanted to meet Dr Nakamura Tetsu in person, a hero and role model in my life whose work I discovered as a student in Japan and that changed my perspective on international development. To me, he was a true incarnation, if not a surpasser, of Yu the Great—a physician-turned-hydrologist who dedicated his entire life to alleviating suffering in a scarred foreign nation based on compassion and a deep penetrating understanding of its local community. Nakamura's story in Afghanistan is less known in the west, perhaps because it was easily overshadowed by the piquant conflicts and military activities of the US forces, ISIS, or Taliban. While empty vessels tend to make the most noise, still water runs deep. Nakamura never intended to impress nor put his work under the spotlight. Despite the war, challenges, and radical changes in externalities, he was able to put his body, heart, and mind into one single cause—transmuting and adapting his strategies along the way without being swayed or affected. As a doctor, all he cared about was to do whatever he could in any given situation, to save as many lives as possible, and thus 'shine light on a corner of the world' (*ichigu wo terasu* 隅を照らす)—a quote he borrowed from Saichō that guided his life through thick and thin.

The Maverick Doctor

Nakamura's beam of light first arrived at the border of Afghanistan and Pakistan in 1978, when he came to ascend the 'King of Darkness' mountain, Tirich Mir, the highest peak in the Hindu

Kush range. Being an avid fan of insects and mountaineering, he quickly developed an affinity for the region's natural environment and people, but was equally aware of its devastating state of poverty. This experience led Nakamura to take up a clinical position in Peshawar, Pakistan, in 1984, where his first endeavour was to treat Hansen's disease or leprosy, a bacterial infection that could lead to nerve damage and sensory paralysis. Many Hansen's disease patients—due to their loss of pain sensation— ended up developing blisters under the soles of their feet, which, if left unattended, could aggravate into plantar ulcers or bone infections that later required amputation. With only himself and a nurse attending to more than seventy patients on a single day, Nakamura was critically undermanned and needed a more cost-effective solution—one that lay outside the traditional box of medical thinking.

Here, Nakamura exhibited his first instinct of creativity and sharp acumen in problem-solving. Noticing how his patients' dilapidated shoes were often mended with nails that posed severe risks to escalating injuries, he reckoned that better quality shoes would change the game. But he avoided merely importing shoes from abroad, for he understood human psychology well enough to know that many poor patients would end up selling them in bazaars unused. Thus, he recruited skilled local shoemakers and commissioned them to make sandals of native origin with added cushioning to be distributed to patients. This not only supported the local craftsmen, but resulted in a dramatic reduction of foot amputations in his ward—a propensity (*shi* 勢) that transcended time and space to affect a positive change in the future.

'What actually provided the greatest boost, though, was not our obvious accomplishments, like surgery or reconstructive treatment, but rather the fact that we opened a shoe shop in the ward,' wrote Nakamura in his memoir *Providence Was With Us*.

Throughout the '80s and '90s, Afghanistan was ravaged by an internecine civil war complicated by Soviet intervention—

displacing large numbers of refugees to Pakistan. As farmers took up arms to fight as soldiers, Afghan villages were split into different factions and the traditional order of a once peaceful agricultural society was torn up. At Peshawar, Nakamura found it difficult to turn down refugees who sought him for medical treatment. The immeasurable scope of death and suffering he saw compelled him to extend his medical work into Afghanistan, first by preparing a series of efforts to build friendly relations with people from the local region, selecting young refugees to be trained as medical staffers, and consecutively setting up two satellite clinics and a hospital in remote mountain villages near the Kunar River region.

The Search for Water

Hasuoka Osamu first went to Afghanistan when he was nineteen and met Nakamura Tetsu there five years into his career as a war correspondent. Honouring the doctor's invitation, at the age of twenty-seven he joined Nakamura's early efforts in setting up medical infrastructures in Afghanistan. Unfortunately, around this time in early 2000, Afghanistan was hit by one of the worst droughts in history, pushing millions into starvation, thirst, and exodus. Misfortunes never come singly.

'The lack of access to clean water translates to the death of countless malnourished babies,' Hasuoka told me in an interview. But Nakamura showed no signs of giving up. He quickly perceived the root of the problem, and immediately shifted his energy towards solving water scarcity. He organized efforts to rehabilitate *karez*, traditional horizontal underground waterways, in Afghanistan and mobilized his staff to dig wells in various locations for drinking and agriculture. 'The fact is, most of the illnesses we dealt with could have been avoided if people had an adequate supply of food and clean drinking water,' the doctor wrote.

Hasuoka (squating on the left) assisting Nakamura with his well-
digging projects in Afghanistan.
Photo courtesy of Hasuoka.

Hasuoka's description of Nakamura conjures the image of a
wrathful deity—a seemingly fierce yet enlightened being who
acts from a source of compassion to help others remove their
obstacles and suffering. 'Dig out 600 wells in the next one
year,' he instructed Hasuoka. 'I don't care how you do it. By
hook or by crook, we must produce water. Clean water.' It
was a stern order. Together with his other colleague, Meguro,
the two protégés accomplished their daunting task. Hasuoka
was in charge of the digging and maintenance of more than
850 wells between the years 1999–2003. 'In the beginning,
we distributed tools and rallied villagers to participate in the
well-digging projects. It was extremely difficult because people
were so poor.' Moreover, the clean-water sourcing projects
coincided with the September 11 attacks and the subsequent

US invasion in Afghanistan to oust the Taliban. It became an
ever riskier and more dangerous situation for Nakamura and
his fellow workers. But together they decided to stay.

'While the US began pouring massive amounts of dollars
into Afghanistan to train mercenaries, Nakamura was tirelessly
travelling back and forth to Japan to raise money and pay locals
to participate in digging wells,' Hasuoka said. Once Nakamura
was invited to speak at Japan's National Diet meeting where he
argued strongly against dispatching the Self-Defence Force to
support the 'war on terror'—suggesting that it would only spark
anti-Japanese sentiments and 'cause more harm than good'.
Instead, he made a solid appeal for Japan to provide famine relief.
Japan's well-known pacifist constitution was what protected
him thus far, he vouched strongly. His speech at the Diet
was immediately faced with intense commotion as right-wing
politicians rushed to mock and ridicule him. Amidst the war, not
everyone in Japan and Afghanistan was kind and understanding.
'There were villagers who deserted us halfway, those who came
just for the "party" and food and, in one instance, an angry mob
even overturned our vehicle. But I've never heard Nakamura
sensei complain a single word.' Hasuoka recalled Nakamura's
stoic personality. 'When unpleasant things happened, all he
said was "it's not important. This is not important."' Rather,
the doctor would find respite in listening to classical music,
especially Mozart.

After four years of hard labour, Hasuoka returned to Japan
to catch a breather. He worked part-time in an antique shop, tried
running his own business, and joined the work of another non-
profit in Sri Lanka to assist in the post-2004 tsunami disaster
rehabilitation as well as in Vietnam to oversee the construction
of a small hospital. Hasuoka's coming of age in Afghanistan
toughened his spirit and widened his horizon to explore the
world. Then one day, upon receiving a rare phone call from
his teacher, he decided to return and help out Nakamura for

another year—his final stint with the maverick doctor. By then, Nakamura had already suspended previous water-sourcing projects and was concentrating solely on The Green Ground Project, a bold ambition to revive self-sustainable farming villages through the construction of irrigation canals from the Kunar River into the desert. 'Underground waters in wells were drying up faster than what Mother Nature could supply. It was helpful in the beginning but it was not sustainable long term. Imagine digging deeper and deeper indefinitely until we hit a limit.' Hasuoka explained.

Nakamura Tetsu standing in the middle with his local and Japanese volunteers. Hasuoka next to him on the right.
Photo courtesy of Hasuoka.

Flowing Water

To materialize the canal, Nakamura and his staff plunged into a long journey of trial and error. He revised his knowledge of mathematics, consulted riparian engineers from Japan and learned from scratch the basics of civil construction—all the while keeping in mind the effects of climate change, the relevance of local topography, and the social conditions in Afghanistan, especially their lack of modern technology and material resources. Whenever he returned to Japan, Nakamura intentionally visited water-use facilities of various types. He wanted to understand how hundreds of years ago—before the advent of boring machines and concrete—his forefathers were able to build waterways from rivers to cultivate their land.

'One of Nakamura sensei's pet phrases was *korewa saisendan da* これは最先端だ "What an advanced (technology)!"' Even if it was just a traditional fixed pulley, a *karez* system, a simple tent or a mud house made by the indigenous people, he was filled with awe and curiosity. In his eyes, he saw sparks of innovation everywhere and was genuinely interested in the stories and people behind those creations. This renaissance spirit connected him to the local people and enabled him to discover some of Japan's ancient wisdom or techniques to be applied in Afghanistan.

The Yamada Weir, a type of oblique weir in which boulders are diagonally arranged across the width of the Chikugo River to divert part of its water into constructed canals, was perhaps the most crucial discovery for Nakamura. Built in the eighteenth century in Fukuoka, it is located on a basin that much resembled the terrain and rough current of the Kunar River in Afghanistan. Nakamura spent the bulk of his time consulting blueprints from the Edo era to reproduce the weir along the Kunar River, while local farmers were entrusted with the work of digging out irrigation canals and solidifying the embankments with traditional Japanese *jakago*, or gabion techniques (large wire containers filled with rocks stacked on top of one another), and the planting of willow trees to reinforce the walls.

A picture map of the Yamada Weir from the Edo period (1757).
Image courtesy of the Asakura City Education Board[2]

'Willow trees grown behind the gabions extend countless roots into the cracks between the rocks and create a "living basket".' Nakamura wrote in his memoir. 'Rather than pushing rocks out of place, their powerful yet gentle growth envelops the rocks, providing further support. [It] is a marvelous plant. Even if submerged, its roots do not rot.'

The reason for choosing such a man-powered traditional methodology was two-fold. The first is sustainability. This method not only provided employment for refugees to return and rebuild their homeland, but also allowed the Afghan farmers themselves, who are adept stonemasons, to maintain and repair the irrigation canals into the future. The second reason is harmony and biodiversity. 'Perhaps the whole project could have been completed much sooner using modern technology,' Hasuoka elaborates. 'However, Nakamura sensei was wary of the damage of artificial concrete

---

2 『上座下座両郡大川絵図』（1757年）「水車物語」掲載、朝倉市教育委員会文化・生涯学習課文化財係提供。

materials to the natural environment, and reduced such usage to a bare minimum. He wanted the people, canals, and farmland to be integrated into Nature. The forested willow trees, for instance, not only help retain water, but act as windbreaks to reduce the force of wind in the desert. At the core of his philosophy lies a deep sense of respect. Respect for the local people, and respect for Nature.'

Nakamura's methodology in Afghanistan relates to Fukuoka Masanobu's proposition for revegetating the desert using a 'plant-based irrigation method'. In *Sowing Seeds in the Desert*, Fukuoka suggested creating green belts along riverbanks as the first vital step towards expanding into the interior. This method 'does not rely on running the river water through concrete waterways, but encourages the water to follow greenbelts of plants . . . Pussy willows, purple willows, and alders will provide protection from the wind, cool the understory, and draw water . . . If we plant every kind of plant, starting from the area around the river, the underground water will filter up the roots of the plants, and gradually a protective forest will develop.'

After seven years of hardship. Nakamura's extensive network of green-belts-channels was materialized in 2010. Throughout this period of time, more than a million trees have been planted. The twenty-five-kilometre long Marwarid Canal, which extends into the Gamberi Desert irrigates more than 16,000 hectares of land, bringing vitality and lush vegetation to where was once dubbed the 'Valley of Death'. Today the Green Ground Project supports the livelihood of more than 650,000 people, which in turn brought stability and peace to the surrounding region. With less crime, less drugs, and better law and order, villagers were busy farming and had no incentives to fight for a living. Nakamura wrote in his memoir:

> American helicopters often passed over the areas where we were working. They fly the skies in order to kill, we dig the earth in order to live. There are pleasures here on the ground that they will never know—the feelings of those who exalt when the parched land obtains water. It is our privilege to witness the

exuberant dance of life in the smiling face of children playing by the river's edge. This is the foundation of peace.

The Kunar region where Dr Nakamura and the staff of the Peace Japan Medical Services (PMS) continued their work despite bombing attacks was dubbed as 'Afghanistan's Heart of Darkness'—one of the most dangerous terrains and no-go-zones anywhere in the world.[3] It became a common occurrence to see US helicopters flying in formation right next to Nakamura's irrigation canal construction sites. The political situation in this mountainous region fell beyond what the news media would like to simply categorize as Taliban-controlled or US-controlled. Rather it was administered by Pashtun tribes who sometimes have family members representing opposing factions but who could easily switch sides based on the winning team.

Nakamura was constantly frustrated with the West's failure to perceive the true configuration of the Taliban and simply labelling them as enemies. The word 'taliban' originally meant 'students', but it had no clear definition. In many places, it is viewed as a social movement, and a lot of so-called 'taliban' were simply respected village elders in Pashtun villages. According to Sawachi Hisae, 'Where there were the militant Taliban, there were also the unarmed Taliban who oversaw the country's agricultural industry. Dr. Nakamura said jokingly, "It wouldn't be wrong to call me a Taliban leader. Most of the Taliban members were simply old folks living in rural communities like me." He said with clear anger in his voice, "They were wrong to conflate the Taliban with terrorism."'[4] Nakamura's deep respect and understanding of the regional custom, language, and tribal Pashtunwali code enabled

---

[3] Brian Glyn Williams, 'Afghanistan's Heart of Darkness,', *CTC Sentinel* 1, no. 12 (November 2008).

[4] Hisae Sawachi, 'The Path that Dr. Nakamura Left to the Afghans: The Water that Saved 600,000 People.' Discuss Japan: Japan Foreign Policy Forum, March 2020, https://www.japanpolicyforum.jp/diplomacy/pt2020033119184310299.html (accessed April 5, 2023).

him to work in one of the most complicated regions of the world, and accomplish the seemingly impossible.

Nakamura's 'Spiritual Legacy'

Hasuoka left Afghanistan after finishing his second stint with Nakamura, and the two men's life trajectories began to diverge soon after. In Afghanistan, Nakamura started the Miran Training Center to pass on his technical knowledge of hydrology to the locals while continuing his effort to aid them in the construction of several major weirs and canals. 'One irrigation canal will do more good than 100 doctors . . . A hospital treats patients one by one, but this helps an entire village,' said Nakamura in the NHK documentary *Water, not Weapons*. One of Nakamura's favourite quotes on the relationship between humans and nature comes from the bible, 'Consider the lilies of the field, how they grow; they toil not, neither do they spin. Yet I say unto you that even Solomon in all his glory was not arrayed like one of these.' Despite being a baptized Christian, Nakamura's heart transcends any narrow constraints of religion to embrace diversity. Once the farms became sustainable, he gracefully accepted the requests of local farmers to help them build two mosques in their villages.

'Nakamura abhorred major conferences discussing peace.' Hasuoka said. 'For him, peace is not a concept, but something to be walked and practiced by each individual, based on their own *minotake* 身の丈—stature, circumstances, or capacity—in his or her own corner of the world. Peace is a by-product of one's work and actions.'

Back in Japan, Hasuoka found his own *minotake* to instil peace through childhood education. He took over a bookstore in Kyoto and converted it into an academy focused on storytelling and the dissemination of children's picture books. This idea came about when he was working in Afghanistan and saw sparkles in the eyes of children who were told stories using children's picture books from Japan. At the end of the day, he was amazed by the curiosity, empathy, and healing that transcended nationality and culture.

Hasuoka-san demonstrating how to read a children's picture book to the author, as well as explaining the idea of a tree ring formation in relation to education

There are many family issues in our society today. I don't think picture books can solve all these problems. However, I do believe in the power of stories from carefully hand-picked picture books, in leaving a lasting impact in the lives of children, and its potential to transform relationships between the listener and the reader.

This is Hasuoka's actionable baby step towards peace. He curates his library collection based on different themes related to human life and recommends picture books to clients, each tailored specifically to a child's age, interest, and development. Each day, his academy hosts ten parent–children pairs. For babies aged up to one year, mothers are taught to communicate stories with their gentle voice, aided with bright colourful picture books to attract the toddler's attention and invite them into an expanding visual world. Children between the age of two and three are told self-affirming stories as they begin to empathize with characters from picture books. This is also a critical period of time to deepen trust between parents and children. Those beyond four and five are gradually exposed to even more imaginative languages and splendid pictures. As they become aware of their own existence and place in society, the right picture books coupled with the right storytelling techniques can help impart teachings of wisdom, grit, and self-esteem.

Hasuoka drew a picture of tree rings and showed it to me. He explained that a picture book is meant to be narrated, its story to be shared between two or more people. Because when an adult narrates a story, not only does the listening child leave a potent mark on its current 'ring' formation, but the inner child within the heartwood of the adult, too, is alive and responding. This idea corresponds with 'zoetological thinking' (*shengsheng lun* 生生論) a neologism coined by sinologist Roger T. Ames to describe a holistic, organic, and ecological view of humans in the process of constant 'becoming' to contrast the western ontological view of just 'being'.

'The dynamics of the radial expansion of the annual rings of a tree is a vital process that over time forms the heart and pith of the tree, and tells the story of its rooted "essence" growth. The sap of the tree—the life force—travels through the inner bark of a tree, which serves as a conduit to circulate, repair, and rejuvenate the root, trunk, and branches." Roger shared with me over a teleconference. 'Each episode in the tree's narrative as told in its rings is unique to its growth, and is incremental to its focal identity. So do we as humans.'

Stories and shared feelings of love nurtured through parent–child interaction can powerfully shape the character of an individual. Like tree saps, they can traverse across time and space to heal wounds and nourish the internal structure that supports our present growth.

'Did Nakamura sensei know that you were inspired by his work and started this social business in Japan?' I asked.

'No. We were rarely in touch with one another.' Hasuoka replied. 'He was extremely busy and was focusing on doing his best to benefit others in Afghanistan, and I guess I was doing the same thing in Japan. We were both trying to live in the "present" moment.' Upon returning to Japan, many of Nakamura's young workers have dedicated their lives to 'shining light in their own corner of the world.' One worked for an organization to help rural farmers share their knowledge with one another, another studied and became a community doctor, and in Hasuoka's case, he was naturally inclined towards becoming a childhood educator and social entrepreneur.

While a cup of exquisite tea may leave behind a joyful, pleasant, and uniquely harmonious aftertaste, *cha yun* 茶韻 in the mind of a tea drinker; Nakamura's Dao of Flow left strong spiritual imprints (*yun* 韻) and a 'reverberating legacy' (*yoin* 余韻) in the hearts and lives of countless Afghans as well as in those young Japanese volunteers who worked under him.

Water, Not Weapons

December 4, 2019, marked a day of utmost despair. On his way to work in Jalalabad, Nakamura was assassinated by unknown assailants, alongside four bodyguards and his driver. This shocking event occurred amidst escalating tension between foreign forces and the Taliban two months after Nakamura was awarded honorary Afghan citizenship by President Ghani.[5] No one has publicly come forward to claim responsibility over the killing.

Hasuoka was shocked when he received the news of Nakamura's passing away. To come to the realization that a teacher is no longer alive in this world takes some time to register. However, another thought that came to his mind was a mixture of awe and admiration. 'Ah what a way to die,' Hasuoka said. 'For someone to have accomplished an amazing feat in a place he loved, for the people he cherished, and to die with dignity. I think Nakamura has lived a good life.' Hasuoka felt an urge to carry on Nakamura's Dao of Flow in Afghanistan and told Peshawar-kai (Nakamura's organization) that he was ready at any time to return and serve if they needed him in the future.

'Do you mind if we grab a meal together the next time I visit Japan?' I asked Hasuoka.

'Of course! Why not?! You're more than welcome to put up at our place in Kyoto.'

'Perhaps through you, Hasuoka-san, I could in a way have a meal with the late Nakamura sensei.' I explained about the prompt and my answer from 'The 36 Questions That Lead to Love.'

Hasuoka laughed. 'Frankly speaking, I don't think Nakamura sensei would be that fun of a person to have a meal with. He is a very strict (*kibishii* 厳しい) fellow, and a man of few words.'

---

[5] Shereena Qazi, 'Why 2019 was Afghanistan's best and worst year since US Invasion', *Al Jazeera*, December 2019, https://www.aljazeera.com/news/2019/12/28/why-2019-was-afghanistans-best-and-worst-year-since-us-invasion (accessed April 5, 2023).

Throughout his life, Nakamura had many brushes with death. When one of Nakamura's clinics came under attack in 1992, he had ordered his people not to shoot even if they suffered fatalities, to prevent a cycle of retaliatory killing. He once narrowly escaped a machine gun firing from American helicopters who mistook him and the group he was with as insurgents, and on a different occasion sewed a bullet wound on his leg without an anesthetic. During a 2010 flood, he risked his life draining water out of a canal in order to save an intake gate from collapsing, thus preventing a huge catastrophe.

'Nakamura sensei was constantly putting his life in danger. He had no regrets, and was prepared to die from the very beginning,' said Hasuoka.

'There is one thing that I can be certain of from my experiences in Afghanistan: I was never protected by military might. Defence does not necessarily depend on weapons,' Nakamura wrote in his memoir. 'The way to touch people's hearts is by showing sincerity to look beyond personal interests, to practice patience, and to not retaliate with deception even when deceived.' His memoir echoes principles from the Dhammapada, such that 'hatred does not cease by hatred, but only by love; this is the eternal rule.' The fact that he was able to survive a war zone for more than three decades, persisted in his endeavours to save lives and to launch the Marwarid Canal with only about 6 million dollars of seed money was nothing short of a miracle, and a testament of his commitment to non-violence.

In contrast, according to Brown University's Costs of War Project, the United States spent 2.3 trillion dollars in Afghanistan from 2001–2022.[6] During the same time period, about 175,000 people died in Afghanistan as a direct result of the war, based on

---

[6] Thomas Howard Suitt, 'High Suicide Rates among United States Service Members and Veterans of the Post-9/11 Wars', *Costs of War*, https://watson. brown.edu/costsofwar/papers/2021/Suicides (accessed April 5, 2023).

the same report. This includes about 70,000 Afghan government
soldiers and police, and about 50,000 each of Afghan civilians
and Taliban. The US death total is a bit more than 6,000. The
majority of them were contractors, with US military deaths of
2,324. It is clear that the vast majority of death and suffering has
been borne by the Afghan people. Among veterans who returned
to the US from service in Afghanistan or Pakistan, many suffered
from PTSD. As of June 2021, the report says that 30,177 veterans
committed suicide.[7]

I often imagine and wonder about the outcome had the
same amount of resources spent in Afghanistan been based on
Nakamura's methodology. What difference would it make if
money was spent on a large scale to assist local Afghans revive their
once self-sustainable farming villages instead of arming civilians
to fight the Taliban? Is Afghanistan really simply 'the graveyard of
empires?' Or is it a case of outsiders trying to do something good
in a place they don't understand, using force to try to achieve their
goals, and triggering a fully predictable backlash? Nakamura has
shown that an alternative 'oasis of goodwill' is possible by flowing
with the Dao.

As I compiled notes from my conversation with Hasuoka on
Nakamura, it brought to mind a famous saying in *Laozi* about
water and the power of softness. Softness in this context is not
weakness or appeasement. It means embracing and becoming
flexible like the water in patiently manoeuvering and pushing a way
out of rigidity, not to mention also nourishing its surroundings,
both literally and figuratively:

> Water is the softest thing in this world,
> yet in penetrating the hard and strong,

[7] 'Human and Budgetary Costs to Date of the U.S. War in Afghanistan, 2001-
2022.' *Costs of War*, https://watson.brown.edu/costsofwar/figures/2021/
human-and-budgetary-costs-date-us-war-afghanistan-2001-2022 (accessed
April 5, 2023).

there is nothing that can surpass it.
Softness overcomes hardness;
Tenderness prevails over strength.
Under heaven there is no one who does not know this.
Yet no one can do it.[8]

Well, not quite. Not everyone understands this. There are some who embody this spirit.

They flow it. And they continue to integrate it within their lives, blossoming as walking flowers. I think Nakamura was one of them.

Can we, too, be like water?

Jin Young finally meeting Hasuoka-san for a meal in person.
Kyoto, May 2023.

---

[8] 「天下莫柔於水，而攻堅強者莫之能勝，其無以易之；弱之勝強，柔之勝剛，天下莫不知，莫能行。」《老子》

Epilogue

What happens when you've reached the mountaintop?

In a cramped room in Beijing, a painter casts a few drops of ink onto rice paper. Her brush splashes. Everyone is bewildered. She allows her intuition to take over the brush, making spontaneous strokes of varying intensity. The patterns unveiled by the random splash and strokes gradually come to evoke potential images of flowers, birds, mountains, or maybe a meditating recluse. I don't know. Neither does she. It was all without a single predetermined intention. Or perhaps there was some imperceptible calculation. That's fine, too. What matters most is that her body, brush, ink, and paper have become one, and she is doing it out of electrifying joy. Like water, she embodies prior imperfections and randomness and flows in search of empty space, each and every step intuitively calibrated with an eagle's eye for untapped beauty. With a few finishing touches, the path and its fruition are beautifully regulated: a white paper transforms into chaos, and through an alchemical play of dark and light, it evolves into a harmonious picture of life, brimming with *qi*, vital energy.

It was in this spirit that Azul Pereda, my Argentinian amiga, created the fish on the front cover of this book. And perhaps, to a lesser degree, I had the same aspiration in inscribing the first two lines of the Daoist classic *Zhuangzi* to complement her painting. The analogy of a Daoist painter seemed befitting for summarizing the three esoteric principles in *The Dao of Flow*. Much of who we are and what we have, as of this moment, is akin to splashes of ink and strokes cast upon life. The dice have been thrown. The ink spilled. The fulcrum now lies in how we embody, flow, and regulate our lives like water to create *harmonia*[1] (*he* 和).

Azul Pereda 'caught in the act'.
Photo taken by author.

Throughout this book, I have described the embodiment of water as *song* 松, referring to the right degree of relaxation of one's body, breath, heart, mind, and environment (including soil, as demonstrated by Fukuoka Masanobu). *Song* is the deconditioning of negative habits and unnecessary exertion—a state conducive to natural integrity and optimal performance. This process is also the foundational phase of knowledge accumulation, wisdom cultivation, and refinement in a particular skill or domain. More often than not, the natural spontaneity and grace one finds in

---

[1] In chapter two, we discussed the Greek origin of harmony, *harmonia*, a state analogous to the 'agreement, concord of sounds'.

a virtuoso are masked by years of physiological conditioning. In Azul's case, the fish painting emerged from a combination of multiple failed attempts, formal art classes taken on Chinese painting, and a delicate aesthetic sense nurtured by her grandfather, Nicolás García Uriburu, an ecological artist who pioneered the use of land art to raise environmental consciousness worldwide.

The flow of water, *liu* 流 is the science of non-resistance. I use the word 'science' here because, like gravity, gradient, friction, and volume affecting water flow, there are many individual factors and social conditions affecting human flow. Human flow requires a rational process of continuous observation, inquiry, experimentation, repetition, and analysis. A Walking Flower[2] is adept at discovering 'openings' and tapping into *shi* 勢—the strategic advantage, propensity, or skilful means in each unique context that leads to effortless action. Scott Rozelle found *shi* in his early childhood interventions to close the urban–rural gap; Lü Zhi in ecotourism, local produce, and sacred mountains to promote community-based conservation; and Nakamura Tetsu in ancient Japanese techniques of weir constructions and embankments to replicate similar irrigation systems in Afghanistan. In Daoist terminology, flow brings one into a state of *wuwei* 無為— effortless action—achieving one's desired outcome without exerting brute force.

Water-regulation or *zhi* 治 is the art of living. It demands the unification of wisdom and compassion as one takes a step back to re-examine the purpose of 'flow' and integrates it into a greater system and purpose. Wisdom allows us to perceive metapatterns; and compassion energizes us to act on them so that we might bring *joie de vivre*, beauty, peace, and fulfilment (*le* 樂) to ourselves and others, including Mother Earth. For instance, David Holley utilized his communication skills to inform the world of what

---

[2] Recall the definition: one who walks the flow and does so naturally and beautifully, like a flower.

was happening on the ground in places like China, South Korea, Kosovo, and Yugoslavia, and how world events shaped the lives of local people. Upon retirement, he continued to share his journalistic knowledge and experience with college students—all with the hope of bridging in-group-out-group divisions. Today, Sanghasena spends twenty hours a day managing Mahabodhi, talking to local political leaders, and teaching meditation and karma yoga—trusting that his local and foreign students will go on to spread *karuna* (compassion) and peace in their own lives. As an accomplished artist, Han Meilin now paints for charity, asking how he could use his art and social influence to help other local craftsmen, folk artists, and marginalized students globally. And finally, Daoist alchemy reminds us of the perspective of 'circulation'—a metapattern of nature. Again, returning to *Laozi*:

> Be a river gorge under heaven,
> One retains perpetual merits, virtue, and strength (*de* 德).
> Returning to the state of a newborn.[3]

What happens when you've reached the mountaintop? You understand the fulfilment of scaling it, you get a bird's-eye view of the surrounding region, you see the location of each village below, the different routes that lead up to the peak, and the liberating experience of touching the sky. But still, after a period of solitude, you realize it's time to descend. You return home, bringing a part of that mountain with you. And with renewed cognizance—a beginner's mind, a newborn—one begins a new cycle of embodiment, flow, and regulation. A new piece of rice paper unfolds before you.

~

---

[3] 「為天下谿，常德不離，復歸於嬰兒。」《老子》

Daoism is a fuzzy word. Some view it as a philosophy, others a religion. As you can see, most quotes in this book, all of which are self-translated unless identified, are heavily drawn from classical texts with connections to Daoist philosophy. However, I also pulled out a few quotes associated with thinkers from other schools such as Confucianism or Buddhism. The categorization of a 'Daoist School of Thought' during the Warring States period in China is often seen as being apocryphal, a later reconstruction of different lineages by later scholars in the Han and post-Han periods[4], and much redaction of these texts has occurred across history. Historians of early China suggest that there has been a continual cross-fertilization between thinkers and masters. What's most important for anyone studying Daoist philosophy (and, I would argue, for most Chinese and Eastern philosophy) is that they demand a sort of personal interpretive engagement. Classical texts are written in classical languages. Each ancient Chinese character could sometimes be a noun, a verb, or an adjective, and connotes a plethora of different meanings. The interpretation of each paragraph is sometimes dependent on one's subjective experiences. This book can thus be seen as my own personal interpretation of the Dao in relation to my life. And as I try to demonstrate here, the wisdom of ancient 'Dao-ists' transcends national, cultural, and spatiotemporal boundaries. It could be embodied in an Indian monk, a Chinese artist, an American economist, or a Japanese doctor; in indigenous communities and urban cities; and in ancient sages as much as modern sapiens.

I hope this book can spark a conversation with yourself on your own interpretation of the Dao, informed by other readings, experiences, and wisdoms you have collected in your life. They flow together. And you embody them. In so doing, I'm optimistic

---

[4] Mark Csikszentmihalyi and Michael Nylan, 'Constructing Lineages and Inventing Traditions through Exemplary Figures in Early China', *T'oung Pao* 89, no. 1/3 (2003): 59–99, http://www.jstor.org/stable/4528923.

that we will create a more harmonious world nourished by our interconnected *Dao of Flow*. I look forward to meeting you at the next crossroads.

'Mountaintop.' A panoramic drone shot of author and his participants trekking in the Himalayas. Drone shot taken by Samuel Wong, a wonderful friend from the Filmmakers Company.

Acknowledgements

This is a very personal book. I owe my existence, growth, and luck to a boundless web of intertwined influences. Thus, fully acknowledging every contributing factor or individual is impossible. I apologize in advance for any omissions, which are no doubt numerous.

I trace the genesis of this book to the spring of 2021 when I was happily stuck at home in Penang with my parents due to the pandemic. Never waste a crisis, I thought. This period of solitude, interspersed with contemplative practices, proved especially conducive to meditation. I naturally found myself dabbling in writing as I began recording some of the most interesting experiences I've had in life. This baby step took me into uncharted wilderness. Each time I finished a short piece of composition, I would eagerly send it to David Holley, who meticulously read, edited, and provided his feedback. Waking up to see David's reply popping up in my inbox was a delightful hit of dopamine and serotonin—a pedagogical experience filled with personal guidance, care, and wisdom that no AI algorithm could ever replicate. Through this back-and-forth interaction, chapters unfurled, and gradually they coalesced into a manuscript. Along the way, David and I have become best of friends, and this book would not have materialized without him nor the support of his wife, Fumiyo.

In the fall of 2021, I hastily left for Beijing to pursue my Master's degree as a Schwarzman Scholar. My writing endeavour extended into China until the end of summer 2023—from Malaysia to my initial quarantine hotels to the stunningly beautiful courtyard of Schwarzman College, and back home again. This fellowship sustained my various projects and opened doors to invaluable mentorships and countless meaningful friendships.

Roger T. Ames has been a beacon of light—a mentor always generous in sharing his profound insights into Chinese philosophy, and the second person to read my whole manuscript. In his loving, articulate, and congenial manner, he taught me the grace of impartial giving and encouraged me to sail ahead, not only as a writer but as an academic. Chade-Meng Tan and Cindy Teo gave me fervent encouragement and constructive feedback—reminding me of the need to always tie my unrestrained tangents back to my narrative backbone. Kimiko Bokura brought me into the wonderful community of Wisdom 2.0 Japan during my senior year at Waseda and has since offered endless support. In China, Song Bing graciously offered me an intellectually rewarding job at the Berggruen Institute, and Wang Hui advised me on my capstone project on taijiquan and holistic education at Tsinghua. Charles Cabell found something special in each chapter, reaffirming the value of putting this book out into the world. Mei Wang from Avenues reminded me constantly to 'ignite the love within, nurture this flame, and shine the world with light'.

As described in the text, I was fortunate to learn from many teachers of contemplative practices who informed my formulation of The Dao of Flow. Among them: Yang-style taijiquan with Chan Yi-Chang at Shih-Chien University, aikido with Seikou Ito sensei in Yokohama, Chinese calligraphy with Lok Pengsan, Pu'er tea with Teh Keng Ee; shaolin and xingyiquan with Ong Ming Thong, yoga with Kosta Miachin, Jason Milne etc., and Buddhist meditation teachers from various lineages—many of whom I shall honour here with 'emptiness'. Of all my teachers, I should single out the mountains and people of the Himalayas. The educational work of Sonam Wangchuk, his Himalayan Institute of Alternative Learning, and especially the Ice Stupa Project, have been an inspiration, and an exemplary act of embodying, flowing, and regulating water. I am most grateful to be blessed with a warm and loving Ladakhi family from Balugun Khampa, Phyang Village, who 'adopted' me and taught me the joy of simply living in harmony with the land and nature. Through them, I learned to *truly see*, and be seen—from the heart.

Our community at Schwarzman College proved indispensable. Will Seaton was an unwavering comrade in peer-reviewing one another's writing. Arjun Sai Krishnan never failed to call week after week to check in on my writing progress. Sameer Dhar read my whole manuscript over one single night and called to tell me where he thought *The Dao of Flow* didn't flow well. Zhi Min Sim greatly uplifted this endeavour as we bonded over our shared Teochew heritage. Annie Sun carefully proofread some of my initial chapters. Chuck Isgar, Eli Morimoto, Oyumaa Daichinkuu, Tony Shu, Ariana Chaivaranon, Miranda Li, Han Yu, Musa Sherif, Habon Ali, Jessie Xu, and Justin Curl read some parts of my manuscript and shared their thoughts. Malik Naibi and Karen Cao provided help and shelter in times of crisis. Eric Muellejans was my partner-in-crime in leading yoga classes for our community amidst lockdown. Yang Hong and Hou Zhi from the Academy of Arts & Design at Tsinghua shared resources and helped with the design layout of my initial manuscript before I submitted it to Penguin, making it much more presentable in its rawest form. Much gratitude to our deans, staff, 6th, and 7th cohort scholars at the college for their support.

I owe heartfelt thanks to my family and relatives. I remember growing up in a three-generation household cradled in the nurturing embrace of my maternal grandmother. I recall her soothing morning prayers, her peaceful presence—feeding grain to the sparrows, gingerly sliding apple slices into my mouth, and guiding my once-tiny hands through layers of crest and folds to craft an origami paper crane. From her, I've come to grasp unadorned beauty and the true meaning of intergenerational friendship. The time I spent abroad, not to mention my upbringing, was made possible by my most beloved mom and dad, and the support of my late uncle, Aun Kheng. My childhood was enriched by the companionship of my dear brother, Jin Way—a true blessing and privilege indeed, to have an older sibling whom I know I could always fall back on in life.

Waseda University was kind enough to support my finances throughout all my undergraduate years when my family most needed it. I am deeply grateful to Dr Victor Wee, my Malaysian mentor, for always rooting for me; and Sharon Yeoh, my first dedicated taijiquan student, with whom I also share an affection for horses. In Japan, Kinuko Umoto, Koya Matsuoka, and Sachiko Matsuoka showered me with unconditional love. Noda Eiichi and Naoyuki Ogi treated me to nourishing meals. Kaori Kohyama called in times of joy and sorrow. Aika Sato unfalteringly brought our circle of friends together on monthly Zoom meetings; she and Aiko Morii kindly read some of my initial writings. Benjamin Yoon and Naoki Harabe remain faithful buddies since our time at Waseda International Student House. A shoutout to two Ladakhi friends, Jigmat Paljor, and Skarma Tsering—both social activists and Mahabodhi graduates—for helping to amplify the outreach of this book.

As I write this from sunny Santa Barbara, I thank Dominic Steavu and our department for enabling me to continue my research in East Asian Languages and Cultural Studies here. Last but not least, I must extend my deepest gratitude to Nora Nazarene Abu Bakar, Amberdawn Manaois, Surina Jain, and the dedicated staff at Penguin Random House for believing in the potential of this book and materializing it. I'm grateful for all those mentioned throughout the book, many of whom I don't repeat here. Thank you for your inspiration, and especially to you, my reader, for engaging in this conversation with me.

This list could go on indefinitely. Writing a book may seem like a solitary pursuit, but in truth, it evolved into a profoundly relational project, a *kizuna* that underscored the significance of communal growth, that we are in a constant state of shaping and, at the same time, being defined by our interconnected relationships.

References

Ames, Roger T. *Sun Tzu: The Art of Warfare*. New York: Ballantine Books, 1993.

Chen, Guying 陳鼓應. *Guanzi Sipian quanshi* 管子四篇詮釋 *(Interpretation of Guanzi's Four Chapters)*. Taipei: Sanmin, 2003.

Chen, Guying 陳鼓應. *Huangdi Sijing jinzhu jinyi* 黃帝四經今注今譯 *(Huang-Lao Silk Texts)*. Taipei: Taiwan shangwu yinshuguan, 2019.

Chen, Guying 陳鼓應. *Laozi jinzhu jinyi ji pingjie* 老子今注今譯及評介 *(Laozi/Daodejing)*. Taipei: Taiwan shangwu yinshuguan, 2017.

Chen, Guying 陳鼓應. *Zhuangzi jinzhu jinyi* 莊子今注今譯 *(Zhuangzi)*. Taipei: Taiwan shangwu yinshuguan, 2020.

Feng, Jicai 冯骥才. *Lianyu·Tiantang* 炼狱·天堂 *(Hell and Heaven): Han Meilin Koushushi* 韩美林口述史. Beijing: Renmin Wenxue Chubanshe, 2016.

Han, Meilin 韩美林. *Qianmian Shi Weizhishu* 前面是未知数 *(The Future is an Unknown Number)*. Jiangsu: Jiangsu Fenghuang Wenyi Chubanshe, 2015.

Lou, Yulie 樓宇烈. *Laozi daodejing zhujiaoshi* 老子道德經注校釋 *(Laozi's Daodejing)*. Beijing: Zhonghua shuju, 2008.

Lu, Yuanjun 盧元駿. *Xin Xu jinzhu jinyi* 新序今註今譯 *(New Prefaces)*. Taipei: Taiwan Shangwu Yinshuguan, 1991.

Lü, Zhi, and George B. Schaller. *Giant Pandas in the Wild: Saving an Endangered Species*. 1st ed. New York: Aperture, 2002.

Nan, Huaijin 南懷瑾. *Zhouyi jinzhu jinyi* 周易今註今譯 [Book of Changes]. Taipei: Taiwan shangwu yinshuguan, 2017.

NHK General TV (NHK総合・津). 'Fukuoka Masanobu (Shizen Nōhōka) [Fukuoka Masanobu (Natural Farmer)].' *NHK Video File: I Want to Meet That Person* (NHK映像ファイル あの人に会いたい), June 1, 2011.

Norberg-Hodge, Helena. *Ancient Futures*. New edition. (East Hardwick, Vermont: Local Futures, 2016).

Putz, R.V. and A.Tuppeck, 'Evolution der Hand', Handchirurgie Mikrochirurgie Plastische Chirurgie, 1999, pp. 357–361.

Rozelle, Scott, and Natalie Hell. *Invisible China: How the Urban-Rural Divide Threatens China's Rise*. Chicago: The University of Chicago Press, 2020.

Shi, Ciyun 史次耘. *Mengzi jinzhu jinyi* 孟子今註今譯 [Mencius]. Taipei: Taiwan Shangwu Yinshuguan, 2009.

Slingerland, Edward. 'Effortless Action: The Chinese Spiritual Ideal of Wu-wei.' *Journal of the American Academy of Religion* 68, no. 2 (2000): 293–327.

Song, Tianzheng 宋天正. *Daxue jinzhu jinyi* 大學今註今譯 [The Great Learning]. Taipei: Taiwan Shangwu Yinshuguan, 2009.

Yao, Chunpeng 姚春鵬. *Huangdi Neijing (shangxia)* 黄帝内经 *(The Yellow Emperor's Inner Classic)*. Beijing: Zhonghua shuju, 2022.

Zhang, Jinghong. *Puer Tea: Ancient Caravans and Urban Chic*. University of Washington Press, 2014.

Zhou, Jianping 周建萍. *Trilogy: Qiafeng Qishi* 恰逢其時; *Meihao Shenghuo* 美好生活; *Guanmen Fuqi* 關門夫妻. Beijing: Huawen Chubanshe, 2022.